The Voice

of the

PROPHETS

Sixteen timely pulpit meditations based on texts from the sixteen Old Testament prophets

---

RUDOLPH F. NORDEN

Concordia Publishing House

Saint Louis

CONCORDIA PUBLISHING HOUSE, SAINT LOUIS 18, MISSOURI

CONCORDIA PUBLISHING HOUSE LTD., LONDON, W. C. 1

Copyright 1963 by Concordia Publishing House

Library of Congress Catalog Card No. 63-20177

MANUFACTURED IN THE UNITED STATES OF AMERICA

To the memory of
RUDOLF M. NORDEN
father, cheerful Christian, and humble country pastor
who faithfully witnessed
to the love of God
in Christ

CONTENTS

[vii]

CONTENTS

PREFACE

The present-day mood of the church is conducive to a devotional study of the canonical writings of the prophets. Like the divinely inspired seers flourishing before the coming of Christ, we are living in crucial moments of history. Far from being serene or describable as an "era of good feeling," these moments are fraught with distresses amid the pains of the birth and death of nations. Walls and dividing lines are in many places separating one world from another. People everywhere are experiencing new tensions and reliving the old. While there is something unique in every situation, there is also a similarity in the pattern of history, a degree of constancy in human reactions to world crises. The truths recorded by the prophets enable us to learn many valuable lessons for application to the parallel circumstances today.

The significant movements of any age have far more than political, economic, and social aspects. Deeply involved in these trends is religion, or man's relationship to God. Technological man's loss of God is unquestionably at the root of many modern problems. Large-scale apostasy was likewise the basis of conflicts engulfing the Children of Israel in centuries past. For that reason the Old Testament prophets had much to say about contemporary events and their inherent future developments. Their messages entailed the pronouncement of divine judgment on offenders, whether heathen aggressors without or the spiritual backsliders within the community of God. The prophets as the living voice of God called God's people to repentance and consoled them with promises of deliverance under the rule of the latter David, the Messiah.

The themes so clearly enunciated by God's spokesmen in the era before the fullness of the time are appropriate for consideration and evaluation today. In this series of 16 pulpit meditations an attempt is made to let relevant texts from the prophetic writings speak to Christians in the 20th century. The old truths are posited, always in the conviction that they are the verbally inspired Word of God, and then placed into the setting of modern living. After the example of the apostles these discourses set forth Christ from the Scriptures as the Son of God and the Savior who died for the sins of mankind, was buried, and rose again. They show how the prophetic Scriptures testified of Jesus Christ.

In offering these sermons to the general reader the author is reminded of Soren Kierkegaard's several volumes entitled *Edifying Discourses*. Kierkegaard was a layman in the Church of Denmark. Having no license to preach, he refrained from calling these messages "sermons," although they are in homiletical form with texts, themes, and the other marks of the sermon. His 1845 volume, *Three Discourses on Imagined Occasions,* for example, envisioned a confessional service, a marriage, and a funeral. Of course, these "sermons" were never preached. They were literary vehicles in which the Danish lay theologian and philosopher unburdened his heart.

Unlike Kierkegaard's discourses, the sermons in this volume were actually preached in Chicago churches, mostly in Christ Lutheran Church, Logan Square, and Bethel Lutheran Church, where the author is pulpit assistant. While attention is given to literary form to please the eye, it should be borne in mind that the presentations were originally orally delivered sermons.

Undergirding the present endeavor is the desire to let the "it is written" of the Old Testament Book edify the church of the New Testament, in keeping with the statement of St. Paul, "For whatsoever things were written aforetime were written for our learning, that we through patience and comfort of the Scriptures might have hope."

THE VOICE OF THE PROPHETS

ISAIAH

When God Removes His Mask

*In the year that King Uzziah died I saw also the Lord
sitting upon a throne, high and lifted up, and His train
filled the temple. Above it stood the seraphim; each one
had six wings: with twain he covered his face, and with
twain he covered his feet, and with twain he did fly. And
one cried unto another and said, Holy, holy, holy is the
Lord of hosts; the whole earth is full of His glory. And the
posts of the door moved at the voice of him that cried,
and the house was filled with smoke. Then said I, Woe
is me! For I am undone; because I am a man of unclean
lips, and I dwell in the midst of a people of unclean lips;
for mine eyes have seen the King, the Lord of hosts. Then
flew one of the seraphim unto me, having a live coal in his
hand, which he had taken with the tongs from off the
altar. And he laid it upon my mouth and said, Lo, this
hath touched thy lips; and thine iniquity is taken away
and thy sin purged. Also I heard the voice of the Lord
saying, Whom shall I send, and who will go for Us? Then
said I, Here am I; send me.*

Isaiah 6:1-8

From time immemorial man has sought God. The
many extant religions mark the various stages of that
search. Every human effort to effect a "breakthrough"
to God has been futile, for God dwells "in a light
which no man can approach unto." The best that man
can do by his own reason and strength as he surveys
God's works in nature is to come to the conviction

[3]

that there is a higher Being, a Creator. Who this God is and what His thoughts are toward mankind must remain a mystery to natural man. There are times when God seems hidden and masked even to His children, as the psalmist remarks with a hint of reproach: "Wherefore hidest Thou Thy face and forgettest our affliction and our oppression?" Similarly Isaiah was moved to say: "Verily Thou art a God that hidest Thyself, O God of Israel, the Savior." When even believers, to whom God has revealed Himself through Word and sacraments, experience what seems to them silence on God's part, how much more is He not remote from unconverted man?

Contact with God is never achieved by the "man in search of God" approach. The reverse is always true: God is in search of man and speaks to him in His Word. In times past, God communicated with His people through holy men known as prophets. Isaiah was one of the prophets *to* and *through* whom God revealed Himself. A very special instance of such a divine self-disclosure is recorded in the text. We give our attention now to this vision, entitling the solemn incident: When God Removes His Mask.

On this, as on other occasions, God revealed Himself as (1) the God of glory; (2) the God of holiness; (3) the God of grace.

I

The God of Glory

In the text Isaiah gives us a written account of an extraordinary happening. An event took place in a given locality and at a given time. The date is indirectly stated thus: "In the year that King Uzziah died." It is at once evident that here we are not dealing with an imaginary experience or a vaguely subjective state of mind. Mere hallucinations cannot be treated in such an objective way. The prophet chronicles a historical event which he *saw*, to which a date is assigned, and of which a detailed report is given. It is like a man discussing something real that occurred — an earthquake, a great medical discovery, or Lindbergh's Atlantic flight — and adding: "I remember it well; it was in the year my father died."

What was the event transcribed in this chapter? The text reads: "I saw the Lord sitting upon a throne, high and lifted up." God appeared to the holy seer in the majesty of a heavenly king. His presence is described as that of a monarch, with flowing robes, attendants, throne, and the like. The setting, however, is not political or secular, but spiritual and churchly. God is seen, as it were, in a magnificent church, for the prophet adds: ". . . and His train filled the *temple*." Later on mention is made also of an altar and of burning coals on it. There is responsive chanting among the seraphim as members of a choir.

From the description we rightly conclude that God is Ruler over His church, which is His kingdom. He is indeed King of the whole universe, the Creator and Preserver of all creation, inclusive of sun, moon, stars, lands, mountains, and oceans. Yet it is principally in the temple, which is His house, that He reveals Himself. The sanctuary is His habitation, His palace, and the place where His honor dwells. Habakkuk announces in the same vein: "The Lord is in His holy temple; let all the earth keep silence before Him."

Temples on earth are, of course, only faint types of God's true temple in heaven. In Ps. 11 we are

[5]

reminded of this: "The Lord is in His holy temple, the Lord's throne is in heaven." What Isaiah beheld was a scene laid in the temple of heaven. This becomes evident as further details are filled in, the first of which is: "Above it [the throne] stood the seraphim." "Seraphim" is a plural noun form derived from a verb that means *to burn.* The suggestion is here of angelic beings clothed in light and the flame of holiness. The seraphim are a high order of throne angels whose fire-purged sanctity answers to the holy light in which God dwells.

The writer proceeds to describe how the seraphim were equipped, namely: "Each one had six wings." The fowl of the air are each supplied with a pair of wings. These celestial beings had three pairs. What did each seraph do with his winged members? Three distinct acts are performed, the first being: "With twain he covered his face." The seraphim give expression to their sense of humility and unworthiness in the presence of their Creator. They cover not only their faces but also their feet, this latter being the second act. The face, as St. Paul would say, is the more comely part of the body and is thus left open to view. In the presence of God, however, the distinction between face and feet is lost. Men and angels must hide them both. We who are sinful men may well learn of the seraphim what it means to show awe, respect, and creaturely politeness when encountering God.

One pair of wings remains. What did each seraph do with it? "And with twain he did fly." What we see is not a still picture, not a tableau, but a moving picture. The seraphim not only stand before the throne but they also fly; they are active. They are creatures of energy, "and they rest not day and night" (Rev.

[6]

4:8). A similar description is given in Ezek. 10, in a vision entitled "The Cherubim and the Wheels."

The scene as depicted so far shows God's throne and the throne angels. It is a picture revealing the majesty and glory of God. All heaven is filled with His glory. What is more, the seraphim say, "the whole earth is full of His glory" also. The glory shown to Isaiah is revealed to us too. We catch a glimpse of it in nature, as the psalmist exclaims: "The heavens declare the glory of God; and the firmament showeth His handiwork." True, this glory breaking through in nature's realm is largely a hidden glory. We know the Creator is there, indeed a glorious Creator, but His face we cannot see. It is obscured behind a mask. Nevertheless there is a measure of glory manifested in creation. Even the unconverted man can know that God is wise and powerful, as Paul emphasizes: "The invisible things of Him from the creation of the world are clearly seen, being understood by the things that are made, even His eternal power and Godhead."

A much clearer revelation God has given of Himself in the Gospel. He reveals Christ as the Way of salvation. In Christ we behold the glory not only of the only-begotten Son but also of the Father. Christ's incarnation, atonement, resurrection, ascension, and other divine acts for our salvation proclaim God's glory and prompt the doxology: "Thine is the kingdom and the power and the glory." Not only in our worship but in all of Christian life as well we must confess as we contemplate so wonderful a salvation: "Glory be to the Father and to the Son and to the Holy Ghost." Jesus, when referring to the Messiah's redemptive works, concludes the discourse by saying: "These things said Esaias when he saw His glory and spake of Him." (John 12:41)

[7]

II

The God of Holiness

In this vision God revealed also His holiness. Special emphasis is given to God's holiness in the text. Isaiah reports not only what the seraphim *did* but also what they *said*. It was this: "One cried to another and said, Holy, holy, holy is the Lord of hosts." The name *Lord of hosts* can also be rendered as *Lord Sabaoth,* that is, the Lord of the armies. According to Rev. 4:8 the six-winged heavenly beings say: "Holy, holy, holy, Lord God almighty, which was and is and is to come." What the seraphim proclaim, along with their testimony of His power, is God's holiness.

Also elsewhere in Holy Scripture God's holiness is underscored. To mind comes the familiar passage "Ye shall be holy, for I, the Lord, your God, am holy." Jesus reechoed this truth in the enjoinder: "Be ye therefore perfect, even as your Father which is in heaven is perfect." God is holy. He is without sin, but that not in a passive sense. He is active and vigorously holy, a zealous God. He hates sin, cannot abide it or compromise with it in any form. His holiness is in direct conflict with evil, as light is intrinsically opposed to darkness.

God is holy, in His nature as well as in His dealings with man. Let us remember this always. If we do not understand His ways with us, we know they are right and righteous. What God does is always in keeping with His holiness, as Moses has written, "His work is perfect, for all His ways are judgment: a God of truth and without iniquity, just and right is He."

The Lord of hosts, so say the seraphim, is holy. They say it not once but thrice. Why thrice? Special emphasis goes with repeating something three times, as when Jesus told Peter three times to feed His lambs and sheep. Undoubtedly there is more here than just a threefold emphasis on the holiness of God. Bible scholars regard the "holy, holy, holy" as a reference to the three Persons of the Godhead, with the quality of holiness applying equally to each Person. The New Testament version of the seraphic statement might well read, "The Father is holy, the Son is holy, and the Spirit is holy."

The revelation of God's holiness has significance for us. We learn of angels the meaning of reverence for the sanctity of our supreme Sovereign. In our world there is waning respect for that which is holy: God Himself, His Moral Law, sacraments, church, government, marriage, the neighbor's property and personal rights, the position of parents at home and of teachers at school. In certain quarters of the inner and the outer city order and discipline are in a state of near collapse. Teen-age children, to say nothing of delinquent young adults, roam the streets in "wolf packs" and attack people. Even policemen are not safe. Teachers in school are in danger of their lives. We have come full circle. In other times and lands pupils — and this was not altogether good — were afraid of their teachers. Nowadays many teachers have reason to be afraid of their students. Why this lack of respect for persons in rightful authority? Is it not because many in our society, children as well as adults, fail to recognize the holiness of God and live as though He had given no Moral Law, revealed no holy will?

It is necessary therefore that we carefully rehearse before the people of this generation the truth of divine holiness. God is not slack concerning His righteous will. He will not tolerate the sin of disobedience and unbelief, but will certainly visit the iniquity of the fathers upon the children unto the third and fourth generation of them that hate Him. He does indeed threaten to punish all that transgress His commandments.

III

The God of Grace

In removing His mask God revealed to Isaiah also His grace and love. In the presence of the holy God the prophet sensed his sinfulness greatly. He moaned: "Woe is me! For I am undone; because I am a man of unclean lips." He was very conscious of the great difference between the holiness of God and the sins that marked him and his people. Here was a sinner, with sinful heart, hands, lips, and eyes, and he had seen the King, the Lord of hosts! The incongruity was overwhelming, as well it might be.

But God had not revealed Himself in the vision to overpower Isaiah or to punish him for his sins. On the contrary, He sought to cleanse him, as the report continues: "Then flew one of the seraphim unto me, having a live coal in his hand, which he had taken with the tongs from off the altar. And he laid it upon my mouth and said, Lo, this hath touched thy lips; and thine iniquity is taken away, and thy sin is purged."

As a man cleansed, sanctified, and forgiven, Isaiah was prepared to be a special instrument in God's hand for a holy mission. Someone must be sent to preach repentance to a disobedient people, and Isaiah was to be that messenger. When God asked: "Whom shall I send, and who will go for Us?" the prophet quickly volunteered: "Here am I; send me." In his role as

[10]

God's spokesman, Isaiah declared not only the sharp judgment of God over sin but also the message of forgiveness, comforting the people with the promise of the coming Savior.

To cleanse all men from sin, God did not send an angel but the King of the angels, His Son Jesus Christ. This King is also the Prophet, proclaiming the Word of God and showing us the Father. Through Christ God spoke to us once and for all. The Son of God was also a Priest, who stepped before God's altar and brought an offering, an offering of His own body and blood for our redemption. By His blood Christ washed us from all sins. He cleansed the whole person, his heart, mind, lips, hands, and feet. These He touched with the glowing coals of divine love, sanctifying all members for His use. What grace!

His servants, as sinners become saints, are now by love constrained to present their bodies as living sacrifices to God. Like Isaiah, we also are called to render a holy service, namely, to spread abroad the Gospel. When the summons for volunteers comes down from heaven itself, "Whom shall I send, and who will go for Us?" we immediately jump to our feet and respond, "Here are we; send us." He has shown such great love to us. We cannot but do and speak the things we have seen and heard. Thus the love of God in Jesus Christ becomes a great power in the hearts of the redeemed, prompting counterlove to Him who first loved us.

Three qualities of God are revealed in the vision Isaiah saw: His glory, holiness, and grace. In the Holy Scriptures God has revealed Himself to us. He makes Himself known that we might know Him, believe on Him, and love Him. To all who by the power of the Holy Spirit find God in the written and spoken Word concerning the Incarnate Word He has removed His mask and revealed the way of salvation. He who is the Way, the Truth, and the Life declares: "This is life eternal, that they might know Thee, the only true God, and Jesus Christ, whom Thou hast sent."

JEREMIAH

The Two Roads

And unto this people thou shalt say, Thus saith the Lord: Behold, I set before you the way of life and the way of death. He that abideth in this city shall die by the sword and by the famine and by the pestilence; but he that goeth out and falleth to the Chaldeans that besiege you, he shall live, and his life shall be unto him for a prey.

Jeremiah 21:8, 9

A MOTORIST REPORTS seeing what he considered an unusual sign in front of a wayside church. The sign was set up in such a way that only one side could be read at a time. The message read: "The wages of sin is death." The motorist mused, "This church has an incomplete religion. It preaches only the Law." On his return trip he had opportunity to read the message on the other side of the sign. The words there were a continuation of the verse in Rom. 6: "But the gift of God is eternal life through Jesus Christ, our Lord." That statement was needed to balance out St. Paul's teaching on Law and Gospel.

People travel in either of two directions in their spiritual journey. The passage each way is clearly identified. One side of the highway marker tells you, "This road leads to eternal life." Go the other direction and you are warned, "This way takes you to

THE VOICE OF THE PROPHETS

eternal death." In our text Jeremiah emphasizes that God has plainly set forth the way of life and the way of death for man's unavoidable choice. He gives us occasion to consider "The Two Roads": (1) The crisis calling for a choice; (2) the difference between the two roads; and (3) the two ultimate destinations.

I

The Crisis Calling for a Choice

In our text are the dreadful words God spoke through His servant Jeremiah. This prophet, often designated the "weeping prophet," lived and labored in the time preceding the Babylonian Captivity. It was a time of tragedy, for king and people in the Southern Kingdom, the Kingdom of Judah, had fallen away from God. Jeremiah was able to foresee the consequences of godlessness and idolatry. In this text he foretells the future fate of Jerusalem. Nebuchadnezzar, king of Babylon, would come to smite many with the edge of the sword and carry others into captivity. When that time comes, Jeremiah warns, none will be spared. Pity and mercy will not be shown, only utmost cruelty.

The prophet cautions: "He that abideth in this city shall die by the sword and by the famine and by the pestilence; but he that goeth out and falleth to the Chaldeans that besiege you, he shall live." Thus Jeremiah's hearers have a choice to make: either to stay in the city and die, or surrender to the Chaldeans and live. This is the way of life and the way of death the Lord sets before the inhabitants of Jerusalem.

We, too, have adversaries. They are greater than Nebuchadnezzar and the Chaldeans, namely, sin and the devil bringing us death and hell. They are more

[14]

to be feared than human enemies, as Christ tells us: "Fear not them which kill the body, but are not able to kill the soul; but rather fear Him which is able to destroy both soul and body in hell." In the presence of the great enemies of the soul God shows us both the crisis and the necessity of making a choice. Confronting us is the issue whether to walk the way of life or of death, the path to Paradise or to perdition.

The choice, as Jeremiah points out, does indeed narrow down to two and only two ways. This we learn also from Jesus, who in the Sermon on the Mount declares: "Enter ye in at the strait gate; for wide is the gate, and broad is the way that leadeth to destruction, and many there be which go in thereat; because strait is the gate, and narrow is the way, which leadeth unto life, and few there be that find it."

The two ways are pictured in the parables of Jesus which contrast two persons. There were two men who went to the temple to pray, a Pharisee and a publican. The Pharisee hoped to be saved by his good works. He fasted twice in the week, gave the tithe of all he possessed, and obeyed many other man-made commandments. Little wonder that he exclaimed in his prayer of self-praise: "God, I thank Thee that I am not as other men are, extortioners, unjust, adulterers, or even as this publican." The second man confessed his sins, threw himself on the benevolence of God, and said: "God, be merciful to me, a sinner." This penitent publican went down to his house justified. We see immediately which man walked the way of death and which the way of life.

All people, whether they are aware of it or not, choose either the way of life or the way of death. There are no middle ways. An accompanist once said to a would-be songstress, "Madam, you don't sing on the white keys; you don't sing on the black keys; you sing in the cracks." That was, of course, an impossible pitch. In one's religious relationships one serves either Christ or Mammon. Man is either for Christ and His cross, and that is the way of life, or he is an enemy of the cross of Christ. He is either for the light or for darkness; he sings either on the white keys or on the black keys.

Only two ways are revealed in Holy Scripture, in keeping with the two doctrines of Law and Gospel. The Law declares: "The wages of sin is death." The Gospel adds immediately: "The gift of God is eternal life in Christ Jesus, our Lord." The way of the Law and the way of the Gospel are placed side by side also in Galatians: "The Scripture hath concluded all under sin, that the promise by faith of Jesus Christ might be given to them that believe." The way of the Lord is clearly marked, namely: "Cursed is everyone that continueth not in all the things which are written in the Book of the Law to do them." The way of the Gospel is described thus: "Christ hath redeemed us from the curse of the Law."

The two roads are indicated also in the fruits, or outcomes. Faith in Jesus Christ yields one kind of fruits, and faith in one's own religion quite another kind. Ps. 1 shows the two contrasting outcomes. The godly man "walketh not in the counsel of the ungodly, nor standeth in the way of sinners, nor sitteth in the seat of the scornful." Instead, "his delight is in the Law of the Lord, and in His Law doth he meditate day and night. And he shall be like a tree planted by the rivers of water, that bringeth forth his fruit in his season." All the while "the ungodly are not so, but are like the chaff which the wind driveth away." In summary, "the Lord knoweth the way of the righteous, but the way of the ungodly shall perish." In the fruits of the flesh and of the spirit, as Paul details them in Gal. 5, are the road of death and the road of life made manifest.

II

The Difference Between the Two Roads

Having seen that there are only two ways, we examine more closely how, according to the Word of God, the two roads are distinguished one from another. We ask first, "What is the way of death?" It had its beginning when Adam and Eve yielded to the improper passion to be like God, and that was the sin of pride. A road sometimes begins with a small, narrow trail and then grows into a broad highway. Sin also grows, develops, widens, and deepens, as James shows: "Every man is tempted when he is drawn away of his own lust, and enticed. Then when lust hath conceived, it bringeth forth sin; and sin, when it is finished, bringeth forth death."

A similar chart of the growth of sin is found in the first chapter of Romans. There St. Paul makes the point: All men have the natural knowledge of God. They know there is a God, that He is eternal, wise, almighty. These attributes of God are known from His works, particularly the creation of the universe. But pagan peoples at the crucial junction took the low road. They took the first step away from God and their inborn knowledge of Him when they decided to go their own way. Step by step they withdrew farther into darkness, very much the way a person descends the stairway into a dark cellar.

How did men make their first break from God? In this way that they "glorified Him not as God, neither were thankful; but became vain in their imagi-

[17]

nations, and their foolish heart was darkened." From that point they went on to "change the truth of God into a lie, and worshiped and served the creature more than the Creator." The third step already involves the judgment of God, man being abandoned and appointed to do what his corrupt heart desires: "For this cause God gave them up unto vile affections." What this shame and vice included is told by St. Paul, namely, unrighteousness, fornication, wickedness, covetousness, maliciousness, and the like. The crowning climax of such a life is also told: "They which commit such things are worthy of death." Here the apostle anticipates the simple equation stated in chapter six: "The wages of sin is death."

God's revelation shows also the way of life, as reflected in the Gospel. Here Christ is the very Center, as He declares: "I am the Way, the Truth, and the Life." The way of life leads through Christ's reconciliation as proclaimed in the Gospel. This is the Gospel which Paul preached, which we received, and wherein we stand.

The way of life in Christ is grounded on definite truth: "that Christ died for our sins according to the Scriptures, and that He was buried, and that He rose again the third day according to the Scriptures." Here we have the first enumeration of the chief doctrines of our faith. The statement was later extended and enlarged into the Apostles' Creed, telling us that "He suffered under Pontius Pilate, was crucified, dead, and buried; He descended into hell, the third day He rose again from the dead." This to a Christian means: "I believe that Jesus Christ . . . is my Lord, who has redeemed me, a lost and condemned creature, purchased and won me from all sins, from death, and from the power of the devil, not with gold or silver,

[18]

but with His holy, precious blood and with His innocent suffering and death."

As we believe, so we live. Having found the way of life in Christ, we walk on it. As Christ is the Center of our justification, so He is of our sanctification. Our life is hid with Christ in God. Our Baptism signifies the new life in Christ, as St. Paul declares: "Know ye not that so many of us as were baptized into Jesus Christ were baptized into His death? Therefore we are buried with Him by Baptism into death; that like as Christ was raised up from the dead by the glory of the Father, even so we also should walk in newness of life."

What is the new life? It is much more than conformity to superficial moral rules. It is much more than preoccupation with incidentals to be avoided, or with a series of "don'ts": Don't smoke, don't drink, don't attend movies on Sunday. The new life has its roots in Christ, for in Him we are a new creation. He lives in us; to Him we have given our entire heart. In us, as in a clean temple, lives the Holy Spirit, whom Christ has sent. If we stand in such a relationship of faith to Christ, there follows, as surely as morning follows night, that we walk in the newness of life. Faith itself and its accompanying sanctification constitute the way of life.

III

The Two Ultimate Destinations

As there are two ways, so there are two destinations, two places where man ultimately arrives. These are heaven or hell. These two destinations answer to the two ways of life previously described. The rich man of Christ's parable fared sumptuously every day. He despised God's Word, loving neither God nor his

[19]

neighbor. What was the consistent consequence of such a life? "And in hell he lifted up his eyes, being in torment." That was eternal death in hell, a fate corresponding to the way of death Dives walked while he was on earth. Death in hell always results from a life of unrepented sin. "Through one man sin entered into the world, and death by sin," the apostle teaches. Similarly, "The sorrow of the world worketh death."

For Christians who walk the way of faith in Christ there is a different destination. We see heaven and eternal life at the end of life's journey. Beyond present homes we see the Father's house of many mansions. To this eternal goal we were pointed when the Holy Spirit through the Gospel convinced us we were on the wrong road. He set our feet on the right road that leads to eternal life.

Our life even now is deeply influenced by the destination to which we are moving. The way of eternal life is the one we walk now, with emphasis on the present as well as on the future. Jesus says: "He that heareth My Word, and believeth on Him that sent Me, hath everlasting life, and shall not come into condemnation, but is passed from death unto life." St. Paul brings the Christian's destination very close when he reminds us that God "hath delivered us from the power of darkness and hath translated us into the kingdom of His dear Son." In other words, the destination is closely related to the present way of life. The Christian's way is always the road of love to God and to his neighbor, and when this love abides in him, he knows he is on the right road, the road that leads to heaven. For a Christian it is not a guessing contest as to whether he will get to heaven or not. His present faith in Christ has already given him eternal life. What remains to be accomplished upon his arrival in heaven is bestowal of eternal life in its fullness.

There are only two roads leading to either of two destinations in the hereafter. On what way are you traveling? You have to make the choice, for to you also the Lord says through Jeremiah: "Behold, I set before you the way of life and the way of death." May we through the Holy Spirit choose life, as Moses from ages past would encourage us today: "I call heaven and earth to record this day against you that I have set before you life and death, blessing and cursing; therefore choose life, that both thou and thy seed may live." Ask yourself therefore, Do I believe in Christ as my only Savior? Do I love Him? Do I love the least of His brethren? If yes, you are on the right road, with the corresponding heavenly destination clearly in sight. God grant us all His power and presence that we may continue on this way until we shall reach our home above.

EZEKIEL

When Bones Became Living Bodies

The hand of the Lord was upon me and carried me out in the Spirit of the Lord, and set me down in the midst of the valley which was full of bones, and caused me to pass by them round about; and behold, there were very many in the open valley, and lo, they were very dry. And He said unto me, Son of man, can these bones live? And I answered, O Lord God, Thou knowest. Again He said unto me, Prophesy upon these bones and say unto them, O ye dry bones, hear the Word of the Lord. Thus saith the Lord God unto these bones: Behold, I will cause breath to enter into you, and ye shall live; and I will lay sinews upon you, and will bring up flesh upon you, and cover you with skin, and put breath in you, and ye shall live; and ye shall know that I am the Lord. So I prophesied as I was commanded; and as I prophesied, there was a noise, and behold a shaking, and the bones came together, bone to his bone. And when I beheld, lo, the sinews and the flesh came up upon them, and the skin covered them above; but there was no breath in them. Then said He unto me, Prophesy unto the wind, prophesy, son of man, and say to the wind, Thus saith the Lord God: Come from the four winds, O breath, and breathe upon these slain, that they may live. So I prophesied as He commanded me, and the breath came into them, and they lived and stood up upon their feet, an exceeding great army.

Then He said unto me, Son of man, these bones are the whole house of Israel. Behold, they say, Our bones are dried, and our hope is lost; we are cut off for our parts. Therefore prophesy and say unto them, Thus saith the Lord God: Behold, O My people, I will open your graves, and cause you to come up out of your graves, and bring you into the land of Israel. And ye shall know that

EZEKIEL

I am the Lord, when I have opened your graves, O My people, and brought you up out of your graves. And shall put My Spirit in you, and ye shall live, and I shall place you in your own land. Then shall ye know that I, the Lord, have spoken it and performed it, saith the Lord.

Ezekiel 37:1-14

A LIVELY NEGRO SPIRITUAL based on this vision of Ezekiel speaks of various bones of the body connected one to another. The human body has more than two hundred bones. When detached, bones are useless to themselves and the body. When properly connected, they become a coordinated whole. This point Saint Paul makes when he urges all members of the body of Christ to fulfill their individual functions, serve one another with their specialties, and thus profit the church. He holds "that there should be no schism in the body, but that the members should have the care one for another."

Not only the church but also the nation can exist only if member states maintain unity. That was a bitter but worthwhile lesson learned in the Civil War. Some states had seceded from the Union. Their armies were defeated in battle, their cities destroyed, their plantations devastated, and their people, as detached remnants, scattered over the desolate scene. The same thing happened to the Children of Israel. When the ten tribes of the Northern Kingdom seceded to go their own way, which was also the way of idolatry, they became spiritual corpses, in fact, denuded skeletons. When the Assyrians carried them away, they became scattered bones. Something similar was to befall the remaining two tribes of the

Southern Kingdom. Nebuchadnezzar had already begun the dispersion by deporting King Jehoiachin and 10,000 leading persons, Ezekiel among them. A few years later he destroyed Jerusalem and led the rest of the people into the Babylonian Captivity.

The vision of the valley full of bones symbolizes the state of God's people as it experienced spiritual death and dispersion among heathen nations. There was, however, to be a revival by the life-giving breath of the Holy Spirit and a reunion under Christ. This hope Ezekiel projects in the vision, which we entitle: When Bones Become Living Bodies. (1) The desolate scene of death and disunity; (2) the means whereby God grants life to men spiritually dead; (3) the hope God fulfills in His people by the miracle of His grace.

I

The Desolate Scene of Death and Disunity

Ezekiel, either in the flesh or out of the flesh, was transported by the Lord to a plain. More exactly, he was taken to "the midst of the valley." What the prophet saw was not a fruitful valley abounding with life. It was more like a battlefield whose casualties were left unburied. The valley was "full of bones." The skeletons were no longer intact but dismembered, with individual bones scattered abroad. The prophet was directed to make a thorough survey of the open valley and to note the great number of bones. His observation also revealed the bones to be "very dry," as the common saying is, "dry as a bone." For so long a time exposed to the sun, the bones were entirely desiccated and, of course, utterly lifeless. The macabre description leaves no doubt that the scene is one of death and disunity.

[24]

The key to the interpretation of the vision is in v. 11: "Son of man, these bones are the whole house of Israel." In better days the Children of Israel were like the body of a healthy man, knit together, coordinated, and alive. Then the sickness of sin set in. Israel's main sin was its rebellion against God. Through unbelief and the refusal to let God be God the members of the body detached themselves from God as their spiritual Head. The disease of sin was followed by spiritual death. With the penalty of death went the process of dismemberment and dispersion.

Separated from God, the twelve tribes of Israel also became separated from one another. The people were aware of this, for the Lord quotes them as saying: "Our bones are dried, and our hope is lost; we are cut off for our parts." The plaint of the faithful remnant, as also Isaiah records it, was: "Zion said, The Lord hath forsaken me, and my Lord hath forgotten me." In earlier times David had described the heavy affliction of the people in similar terms, namely: "Our bones are scattered at the grave's mouth, as when one cutteth and cleaveth wood upon the earth."

The vision of the valley full of bones is a most graphic picture of all mankind in its condition of spiritual death. Nothing could be so the tokens of death as "dry bones." The state of natural man cut off from God is vividly depicted in the text. St. Paul tells the Ephesians: "Ye were dead in trespasses and sins." The word *death* asserts the absence of life. *Spiritual death* rules out the existence of even the faintest scintilla of spiritual life. In his natural condition man is a spiritual corpse; even worse, he is a jumble of dry bones. He cannot of his own strength

[25]

rally himself to rise from spiritual death. What natural powers he has he uses to do works corresponding with his nature, namely, sinful works that further separate him from God.

The typical man of the world refuses to accept the fact of his spiritual death. He is apt to consider himself very much alive. If success came his way, others may say it of him also. At a presumptuous funeral, which saw a vulgar man of wealth supposedly buried as he sat in his Cadillac, an impressed bystander is said to have remarked, "Man, that's living!" In similar delusions the works of spiritual death are often confused with the works of spiritual life. But indulging oneself in sinful pleasure is not living. It is sinking deeper into spiritual death, as St. Paul says of the profligate widow: "She is dead while she liveth."

The vision of Ezekiel is a study not only in death but also in utter disorganization. Man's sin always results in disunity, primarily in that the sinner becomes disunited from God. If anything describes the secularistic, post-Christian person of modern times, it is his isolation from God. The loss of God means also man's loss of his fellowmen, his separation from meaningful human fellowship. When the prodigal young man of Christ's parable parted company with his father, it was not long before he found himself alone in the field. Nothing contributes more to loneliness, to man's loss of himself amid the masses of mankind in modern society, and to the disintegration of the human family than the individual's severance from his God. The field of dispersed bones Ezekiel saw represents the ultimate in man's estrangement from his heavenly Father.

II

The Means Whereby God Grants Spiritual Life

The road to spiritual life and unity is the road that leads back to God. Through Ezekiel God shows us how the process of death and disunity is reversed. The first marker indicating the road back to God appears in the text. That marker looms in the question in which God suggests the possibility of the return of life. The question God asked of Ezekiel was: "Son of man, can these bones live?" The inquiry is anticipatory, in that it implants in the addressee the first thought of the exercise of divine power. Not dissimilar was the question Jesus addressed to the patient at the pool of Bethesda: "Wilt thou be made whole?" Under the shell of the words is the kernel of the real question: "Do you think that God can do what man, even in his wildest dream, considers impossible?" How does Ezekiel react to the Lord's suggestion? He replied, in supreme deference: "O Lord God, Thou knowest." He is willing to leave the matter to God, convinced that all knowledge and all power reside in Him.

Following Ezekiel's answer, the second marker of the road back to God appears, plain in its direction. The Lord commanded the prophet: "Prophesy upon these bones and say unto them, O ye dry bones, hear the Word of the Lord." The directive states in effect: "Preach to the dry bones; deliver a message to them." Many a preacher would have hesitated at the thought of addressing the Word of God to inanimate objects. What is the sense of it? Bones have no ears to hear, no hearts to consider the Lord's message. For the same reasons God's spokesmen today find no great pleasure speaking to empty church pews. Like bones, stones, and sticks, church pews are soulless and cannot hear. However, if God were to command explicitly, "Preach to these empty benches!" no obedient man of God would refuse. God can make also wood and stone respond to His power. He could have raised up seed unto Abraham from dead stones.

Pursuant to God's command, Ezekiel began his sermon to the dry bones. The message God wanted conveyed through his mouth was this: "Behold, I will cause breath to enter into you, and ye shall live. And I will lay sinews upon you, and will bring up flesh upon you, and cover you with skin, and put breath in you, and ye shall live; and ye shall know that I am the Lord."

The Word of God communicated by the prophet had all the power of a divine fiat of creation. It was like the Word by which God said in the beginning: "Let there be!" Even while Ezekiel spoke, a stirring began. Amid a clatter of objects striking objects, the bones assembled themselves into a human structure, like pieces of a jigsaw puzzle falling into their right places. The assembled bone structures were clothed with sinews, flesh, and skin. What an amazing phenomenon!

The unification of the bones was effected, but there was as yet no life, no breath in the reincarnated skeletons. By another direct order Ezekiel was to say: "Come from the four winds, O Breath, and breathe upon these slain that they may live." The address was to the Holy Spirit, the Breath of God, the Lord and Giver of life. The effect was again immediate: "The breath came into them, and they lived and stood upon their feet, an exceeding great army."

The great miracle of turning bones into living bodies was accomplished by the Word of the Lord and by the Holy Spirit working through the Word. This Word, through the ages, has lost none of its power. It is still the means whereby God raises up the spiritually dead and makes them alive unto Jesus Christ. This is the Word of the Gospel which God's prophets preach today and which today is the power of God unto salvation. Our Lord's command is still, in the face of a world full of dry bones that bespeak its spiritual death and disunity: "Prophesy," or "Preach the Gospel." Prophesy to men dead in sin and scattered as human remnants across the world that Jesus Christ is their Life, that He was delivered for their offenses and was raised again for their justification!

The Gospel proclaims that the Son of God came into the world to save, to serve, to gather, to rebuild. Ezekiel prophesied of Him later in this chapter, speaking of the Messiah as David's Servant, namely thus: "David, My Servant, shall be King over them; and they all shall have one Shepherd." The same truth was proclaimed in an earlier chapter: "I will set up one Shepherd over them, and He shall feed them, even My Servant David; He shall feed them, and He shall be their Shepherd." The "Servant David" is, of course, not the long-deceased King David himself, but is David's Son and David's Lord, even Jesus Christ. In John 10 Jesus clearly applies this prophecy to Himself. He identifies Himself as that Good Shepherd who will unite the scattered sheep of God's flock.

Jesus Christ is the Heart and Center of the Gospel: Jesus, who laid down His life on the cross, that through death He might give life to all mankind. This Lord Jesus we preach to men dead in trespasses and sins. This is the Word of whom the Word of the Holy Scriptures testifies. This is the means through which the Holy Spirit awakens the dead, creates faith, and

[29]

gives life. What a miracle of divine grace it is when by the power of God's Word and His Holy Spirit the dead arise and live by faith in Jesus Christ! It is no less astounding than when in a literal sense the bones of a battlefield turn to living, breathing human beings. Is Christianity true? Does the Word of God have miraculous power? Is faith in Jesus Christ worthwhile? Consider the power of the Gospel that changes spiritual skeletons and corpses to people serving the living God. That is your answer.

III

The Hope God Fulfills in His People

A common saying is, "Where there is life, there is hope." The drama enacted in Ezekiel's remarkable vision was meant to instill hope into the dispersed remnants of God's people. The message of hope was announced in these explicit terms: "Behold, O My people, I will open your graves, and cause you to come out of your graves, and bring you into the land of Israel." This promise God fulfilled when at the close of the Babylonian Captivity He brought back a remnant of the people to Palestine. Of course, the ten tribes once consituting the Northern Kingdom never returned, they being absorbed by the populations of the Assyrian Empire. They lost their identity, and no trace of them remains. It was of the two tribes of the Southern Kingdom that a representative group was restored to the Land of Promise to rebuild Jerusalem, erect the temple, and re-institute the worship of God. God wanted His people back in the Holy Land, for there, according to the prophecy of Micah, the Savior was to be born.

It is true: The glory that was Israel's under the

reign of David and Solomon was never to be regained. Such national and political restoration was not necessary, since the hope of revival and reunion was henceforth to rest on the emergence of a new spiritual Israel under the gracious governance of the Messiah, the Servant David. The new spiritual Israel issuing in the New Testament church was not a consolation prize but represented the true people of God whose ultimate home is heaven. The blessings mankind needs above all and upon which its hope of heaven depends are dispensed by the Messiah. In fulfilling the role of Servant and Shepherd He was to unify the flock of God.

In initiating the Kingdom whereby the new spiritual Israel was founded, Jesus Christ, in the full conviction of His identity as the Messiah, chose twelve apostles as reminiscent of the heads of the twelve tribes. These He sent forth on their mission to rally the house of Israel and to enlarge it by the inclusion of Gentiles. By their mouths our Lord proclaimed to His people: "Your graves are opened!" You are released from the bonds of sin and death and granted liberty and life!

In making this announcement to the scattered elements of God's people, the apostles gave due prominence to the doctrinal basis of the Good News, namely, to the resurrection or the open grave of Christ Himself. The resurrection made it possible for the new spiritual Israel to come into existence. Because the Shepherd, slain for the life of His flock, emerged from His own grave, He is able to gather into one the lost sheep from the house of Israel and those "other sheep" from among the Gentiles. This is the hope God fulfills in His people, however afflicted, sore oppressed, by schisms rent asunder and by heresies distressed. With every promise of hope He gives also the promise of its performance, that by His mighty acts all may know He is the Lord.

When was the era of hope to begin? It had its inception when the Breath of God was released upon the world in an unprecedented manner, namely, when the Holy Spirit was poured out on Christ's disciples without measure on Pentecost Day. Peter, on that occasion, realized that the Pentecost event was the fulfillment of what Joel had foretold, that is, the outpouring of the Spirit upon all flesh, on sons, daughters, old men, young men, servants, handmaids, and all members of the household of God. The Pentecost event is also anticipated in the promise God announced through Ezekiel that He shall put His Spirit into His people and they shall live. The New Testament church as the new Israel had its beginning when the Lord performed what He had promised.

Today there are still many nations in exile, in captivity, in a state of division. They are dismembered by dictated peace treaties or held in subjection by communist regimes. It is quite probable that they will never regain their former national glory or their independence. Yet there is hope to sustain God's people. The faithful are members of a kingdom that comprehends all kingdoms, of the Kingdom of Grace, which continues to flourish when haughty empires lie in dust. This is the kingdom over which Christ rules as Servant and Shepherd, as King of kings and Lord of lords. To His people in many captivities God causes His prophets to inspire hope with the sure promise of life and unity in the Kingdom of Grace and the full performance of that promise in the Kingdom of Glory. Ezekiel's vision proclaims the Gospel of hope to all held in bondage behind Iron, Bamboo,

[32]

and other curtains. All shall know, the conquerors and the conquered, that He is God.

While the lesson of the vision is clearly the promise of the spiritual resurrection of the people of God, it is not beyond the implications of it to speak also of the resurrection of the body. The resurrection of the body is promised to all who participate in the spiritual, or first, resurrection. How vividly the vision sets forth the forming of bones into living bodies! This, in a literal sense, shall take place on the Last Day. All who are in their graves and outside of graves shall hear His voice and come forth. Upon dry bones and on the more disintegrated substances of dust and ashes God will lay sinews, flesh, and skin, and will breathe the breath of life into them. It seems so impossible? Remember, then, that God once breathed into lifeless earth and of that clod formed Adam. Is it too hard for Him to do it again? With God nothing is impossible. Through the words of Job He sounds this keynote of hope: "I know that my Redeemer liveth and that He shall stand at the Latter Day upon the earth. And though after my skin worms destroy this body, yet in my flesh shall I see God; whom I shall see for myself, and mine eyes shall behold, and not another."

DANIEL

Golden Image or God?

Then Nebuchadnezzar in his rage and fury commanded to bring Shadrach, Meshach, and Abednego. Then they brought these men before the king. Nebuchadnezzar spake and said unto them, Is it true, O Shadrach, Meshach, and Abednego, do not ye serve my gods, nor worship the golden image which I have set up? Now if ye be ready that at what time ye hear the sound of the cornet, flute, harp, sackbut, psaltery, and dulcimer, and all kinds of music, ye fall down and worship the image which I have made, well; but if ye worship not, ye shall be cast the same hour into the midst of a burning fiery furnace; and who is that God that shall deliver you out of my hands? Shadrach, Meshach, and Abednego answered and said to the king, O Nebuchadnezzar, we are not careful to answer thee in this matter. If it be so, our God whom we serve is able to deliver us from the burning fiery furnace, and He will deliver us out of thine hand, O king. But if not, be it known unto thee, O king, that we will not serve thy gods nor worship the golden image which thou hast set up.

Daniel 3:13-18

MANY OF THE JEWS brought as captives to Babylon attained positions of leadership in government. The outstanding example of such attainment was Daniel, whose pious wisdom brought him promotions under several regimes. King Nebuchadnezzar made him, according to the prophet's own account, "ruler over

[34]

the whole province of Babylon and chief of the governors over all the wise men." Three other Jews who became prominent in government service were Shadrach, Meshach, and Abednego.

The Jews were the people of the Book. The Bible, where it is treasured, always fosters learning and culture. Appreciation for the Word of God prompts the founding of schools where the Word is taught. Men and women devoted to the learning of the Book stand head and shoulders above their less literate neighbors. Largely because of their good education, leading Jews imported from Palestine were able to render public service in the pagan society of Babylon.

A career in public life entails professional hazards. There come temptations to compromise personal integrity. If one's religion is alien to that of the resident majority, tensions are sure to arise. At state functions the official religion of the majority will be invoked, making it necessary for those of a minority faith to decide whether to compromise their convictions or to become open dissenters. An instance of such religious conflict involved Shadrach, Meshach, and Abednego, as Daniel, himself a religious nonconformist, records in the text. The situation confronting the three heroic men resolved itself into this alternative: Golden Image or God? (1) What the choice involved; (2) the blessedness of those who let God be God.

I

What the Choice Involved

Daniel's three friends found themselves in a genuine dilemma. The crisis developed when King Nebuchadnezzar erected a high image of gold and ordered all ranks of public officials to be present for the dedication. The master of ceremonies briefed the august assembly on procedure. At the sound of the music, he said, all must prostrate themselves before the image. All did, except the three Jewish conscientious objectors. They would not bow down. Word of their refusal was immediately sent to the king. Individuals given to feelings of nativism and anti-Semitism would gleefully see to that. Nebuchadnezzar summoned the accused and demanded to know whether the charge were true. He asked: "Do not ye serve my gods or worship the golden image which I have set up?" The inquiry tells us more about the nature of the dedicatory rite, namely, that it definitely involved the worship of idols. The accused in their reply spurned the threat of death in the fiery furnace and simply said: "We will not serve thy gods." They regarded the point at issue as a choice between the golden image or God. They chose God.

How real was the choice? Some will say, "The three Jews made things unduly hard for themselves. They could have regarded the whole thing as primarily a civil ceremony, made a show of obedience to satisfy the king, and conformed outwardly without really putting their heart into it." Shadrach, Meshach, and Abednego did not see it that way. They believed one should not participate in worship unless one meant it and could do it without duplicity, without mental reservation. Their consciences told them it was wrong to adore the gods of Babylon; wrong to engage in actions which others interpreted as worship; wrong to offend the true God by bowing before idols. Yes, the three men had a real choice to make, a choice in which they rightly discerned the issues.

That the choice was real is evident also from a consideration of its consequences. Conformity would have been the easy way out. There would have been

no scene. As conformists they might have put themselves in line for the king's favor and political promotions. In view of these possible consequences, a yes
would have been a moral coward's response to the
king's command to idolatry. To say no involved
consequences too, namely, royal disfavor, destroyed
political careers, if not the loss of their very lives.
Shadrach, Meshach, and Abednego would have been
less than human had they not weighed the consequences of their decision, both pro and con. They
had the courage of their convictions to reject political
opportunism and to do what was right in the sight
of God. This is the position they took: "We shall
remain loyal to God and let the chips fall where
they may."

How real is the choice between golden image or
God today? Very real. We must not be beguiled into
thinking that with the passing of the ancient gods
the dilemma is removed. In America different religions and religious differences prevail. What is more,
there are serious differences within Christendom, differences which involve the truth of God's Word, the
confession of faith, one's relation to God, and the
sacredness of conscience. Almost everyone will at
some time or other become involved in these issues.
Shadrach, Meshach, and Abednego teach us to act
according to the plain Word of God when such situations arise in private and public life.

The choice is real, for gross idolatry is not dead.
Although we may not see many idols in our country,
some of our fellow citizens still believe in false gods.
When at a public occasion "God" is invoked in the
presence of Christians, Jews, Mohammedans, Masons,
Unitarians, deists, and humanists, is it not the "God
in general," the "God" of American democracy, the
"God" who is vaguely acknowledged as Supreme

Being? In order not to offend other religionists, who
are American citizens too, Christian chaplains at such
functions are tempted to invoke "God" rather than
the Triune God and to omit any reference to Jesus
Christ. When in settings where there should be no
prayer at all men pray to "God," are they not invoking
a composite god who does not exist? Is this not gross
idolatry?

Then there is fine idolatry, which puts Mammon
in the place of Jesus Christ, gold in the place of God.
The spirit of materialism, with the marketplace as
its temple, bids incessantly for the heart's devotion.
It says to people great and small, "When you behold
the image of gold; when you see crowds of people
entranced by the glamor of the Almighty Dollar; when
you hear the music of receipts rung up on cash
registers; when you consider all that money can buy,
prostrate yourselves before me and serve me." Materialism, sometimes appearing in the raw and sometimes "made up" with the cosmetics of religiosity, is
the "this world" philosophy. Its creed declares, "A
man's life *does* consist in the abundance of things he
possesses."

The god Materialism is closely allied with a twentieth-century "deity" now in rapid ascendancy,
namely, Technology. There is a distinction to be
made between technology as a servant and Technology as a god. As a servant, technological skill has
brought amazing benefits to mankind. It creates
machines to relieve the tedium of labor, affords conveniences to make life more pleasant, eases pain and
cures sicknesses, opens many new avenues of activity,
and widens man's horizon in many ways. We are
indeed thankful to God for the many scientific ad-
vancements making possible a better life.

[38]

It is, however, a far different role that technology plays when it elevates itself to deity status. It becomes a god when men look to it to solve the problems of the human spirit or regard it as the source whence all blessings flow. Then technology becomes a competitor of God. Then it takes the glory away from God, who is the real Giver of every good and perfect gift, and bestows it on human genius. When people in a technological society become the servants of the machine with its buttons, blinking lights, dials, and gauges, they are in effect bowing down before it and surrendering their souls.

Of kindred mind with the spirit of materialism is the spirit of carnal pleasure. The latter also goes under the name of hedonism. When society becomes affluent, it has at its command two important items: money and leisure. It has then reached a critical stage in its development. The question arises, What shall people do with their superfluous treasure and time? Hedonism at this moment is ready to declare a Roman holiday. Amid an atmosphere of the carnival it sets up its booths and beseeches all, "Come, enjoy yourselves. Eat, drink, be merry, try your luck at games of chance." These cries do not go unheeded, for in prosperous eras people have the wherewithal to indulge. The increasing rate of alcohol consumption, the greater demand for base entertainment, the mushrooming growth of gambling parlors, the accelerated production of salacious literature and films — all are indications of the homage man pays to hedonism.

When we survey the many aspects of fine idolatry, we have reason to know that there are many gods in the land, all trying to draw man away from the true God. Hardly a day goes by in which a Christian will not be confronted by the necessity of choosing whom he will serve, whether Mammon or Christ, gold or God. The choice, as with Shadrach, Meshach, and Abednego, is not always easy. Hard thinking is demanded in order to discern the principles at issue. Always there is the temptation to take the easy road, to follow majority behavior, to select the course of expediency. There are consequences to consider. The decision for God may cost a person many things: his job, favor with man, the ease of life, and life itself. Loyalty to God, while it is the Christian's only choice and one he will make for its own sake, entails not only sacrifices at times but also, as we learn from the case of Daniel's three friends, the blessing of God.

II

The Blessedness of Those Who Let God Be God

Shadrach, Meshach, and Abednego had learned well the First Commandment: "Thou shalt have no other gods before Me." They were convinced that the God of Israel, who had entered into a covenant of grace with His people, is the one true God. This God, so their faith persuaded them, had every right to lay claim to them, body and soul. By giving all their love and loyalty to God, the three embattled men let God be God. This was the only consideration that mattered. Whatever the results, they were in God's hands. And the results were for all to see. They reflect the blessedness of those who amid "many a conflict, many a doubt, fightings and fears within, without," keep their relation to God inviolate. How did the three faithful Hebrews manage to retain their spiritual integrity in the face of such great opposition?

We must go back to Nebuchadnezzar's rage and fury, which were rapidly approaching hot-furnace temperatures. In his aroused emotions the king said, in effect: "How dare you oppose yourselves and the will of your God against my wishes?" In his anger he brought up two points. One was the threat of painful execution. He underscored the terror, calling the place of torment, in a heaping of adjectives, "a burning fiery furnace." In his other point he expressed disdain for God, as Pharoah of Egypt had done before him: "Who is that God that shall deliver you out of my hands?"

Shadrach, Meshach, and Abednego make no long defense, being not concerned to answer the king in this matter. Briefly they say, "Our God whom we serve is able to deliver us." Note the words "is able." The accused do not go out on a limb by saying that God *will* save them from a fiery death, pointing out that He *can* do so, for He is almighty. Without specifying the *how* of deliverance, whether through suffering or without suffering, they further confess their confidence that God will free them from the king's hands. Then came the ultimatum, the final word: God sparing them from the fiery furnace or not, "we will not serve thy gods nor worship the golden image." The reply reflects essentially the same faith Job confessed: "Though He slay me, yet will I trust in Him." It is the faith St. Paul expressed: "We know that all things work together for good to them that love God." This is letting God be God.

How do Christians today put God uppermost in their hearts and lives? They do this by simply acknowledging the fact that God by His great acts in their behalf is their Lord and Father. The first act whereby God expressed love and invites our love in return is creation. God gave us body and soul as outright grants of His favor. Life cannot be attributed to chance, to accidental interaction of energy

[41]

and matter, to nature, not even to parents, who are but God's instruments. Life is a divine gift, as the psalmist declares: "With Thee is the fountain of life." The life God bestowed He also preserves through benign providence. From His hand comes a multitude of blessings to sustain life. The believers' knowledge of this leads to thanksgiving and service. When we say "Thank You" to Him in word and deed, we let God be God, realizing that all blessings flow from Him.

Man lets God be God when he turns to Him for salvation. He cannot be his own savior from sin and its effects. It is no use to try, for all efforts at a do-it-yourself program of salvation fall far short of accomplishment. It is not only useless but also presumptuous for man to "play God" in this respect. To obviate man's attempt to enter His realm, God became man and entered man's realm to gain salvation. Through the incarnation of His Son God came down to mankind in love. God gave His very own Son that through Him He might reconcile sinful man to Himself. Through the atonement, effected by the shed blood of the Son and sealed by His resurrection, mankind is redeemed from sin and enlisted for loving service. When by faith in the Son man accepts redemption, he lets God be God and thus finds bliss in fellowship with Him.

Did Shadrach, Meshach, and Abednego believe in the Son of God, the promised Messiah? We have referred to them as Daniel's close friends. We can be sure they were also Daniel's associates in the faith. Daniel repeatedly prophesied of the Messiah, speaking of Him as the "Son of Man" to be anointed by the Ancient of Days with divine power and glory, to be "cut off" in death, and then to be raised again as the Prince of Life. Through these events, according to

[42]

Daniel's teaching, was spiritual Jerusalem to be restored and rebuilt "unto the Messiah, the Prince." This faith in the expected Christ was most assuredly shared by Shadrach, Meshach, and Abednego.

Christians let God be God in acknowledging not only their divine creation and redemption but also their sanctification. The Holy Spirit through the means of grace sanctifies, enlightens, and energizes them for holy services to God and man. God's children are thus enabled to live for God amid life's ups and downs and the great conflicts of faith, such as the three men experienced. By virtue of divinely wrought sanctification they play the role of God's servants — God's stewards — committing all they are and have to the glory of God and the extension of His rule on earth. As did the three men of the text, they serve God through their vocations or earthly callings, letting God's Word guide them to faithful performances and God-pleasing decisions.

Letting God be God in all affairs of faith and life results in true blessedness, in an abundant outpouring of God's love. Shadrach, Meshach, and Abednego experienced this in a special measure when God performed an astounding miracle to deliver them from death and to restore them to positions of honor. The arm of the Lord is not shortened in our day. If it is His will and our good requires it, God will do mighty works today for the bodily deliverance of His people.

Also with those martyrs of faith that are not so dramatically snatched from death God keeps faith, preserving not only their souls but their entire being for eternal fellowship with Him. Blessed are all martyrs, because of their example to us, their testimony to the world, and their own goodly heritage in heaven!

[43]

Blessed is the glorious company of the prophets and the apostles; blessed is St. Stephen; blessed are the blood witnesses of all ages; blessed are the heroes of faith slain by today's communists; blessed are Dietrich Bonhoeffer and other confessing Christians whom Hitler's henchmen executed! They let God be God, regardless of the cost.

Because three men resisted an entire kingdom and stood up for God, even King Nebuchadnezzar was moved to say: "Blessed be the God of Shadrach, Meshach, and Abednego!" Will even our erstwhile enemies praise God because of our faithful witness? The choice between the golden image and God confronts everyone today in one form or another. May God help us always to prevail in every temptation and trial, so that even the world must exclaim, "His is the kingdom and the power and the glory." Yes, as St. Paul wrote to the Ephesians: "Blessed be the God and Father of our Lord Jesus Christ, who hath blessed us with all spiritual blessings in heavenly places in Christ . . . that we should be holy and without blame before Him in love."

HOSEA

The Door of Hope

Therefore, behold, I will allure her and bring her into the wilderness, and speak comfortably unto her. And I will give her her vineyards from thence, and the Valley of Achor for a door of hope; and she shall sing there, as in the days of her youth, and as in the days when she came up out of the land of Egypt. And it shall be at that day, saith the Lord, that thou shalt call Me Ishi; and shalt call Me no more Baali. For I will take away the names of Baalim out of her mouth, and they shall no more be remembered by their name. And in that day I will make a covenant for them with the beasts of the field and with the fowls of heaven and with the creeping things of the ground; and I will break the bow and the sword and the battle out of the earth, and will make them to lie down safely. And I will betroth thee unto Me forever; yea, I will betroth thee unto Me in righteousness and in judgment and in loving-kindness and in mercies. I will even betroth thee unto Me in faithfulness and thou shalt know the Lord.

Hosea 2:14-20

AMONG WORDS INCLUDED in the everyday vocabulary of people who are influenced by existentialist philosophy are "anxiety" and "despair." *Anxiety* can befall anybody, also the Christian. *Despair* is experienced by those who have passed beyond anxiety to a condition of hopelessness. When man is cut off from God, there is nothing to sustain him in life's crises. He sinks easily then into deep mental depression. Despair

[45]

becomes a grave spiritual problem when it leads people to think there is no forgiveness for their sins.

In the Bible, right in the beginning, we read of Cain, who in a fit of jealousy slew his brother Abel and thus shed innocent blood. When God confronted him with his crime, he replied that his sin and its punishment were greater than he could bear. That was despair. In the New Testament we come upon Cain's counterpart, who likewise was responsible for shedding innocent blood. He was Judas Iscariot, who betrayed his Lord for thirty pieces of silver. Overwrought by his accusing conscience, he had no hope for forgiveness. In despair he went and hanged himself.

In the history of the Children of Israel there were times of widespread despair. In such periods of crisis God raised up prophets to comfort His people. While these spokesmen heavily underscored sin as the cause of spiritual bankruptcy, they never failed to point out the penitent return to the God of mercy as the only way to a life of hope. Our text from the prophecy of Hosea abounds in picturesque expressions of the mercy of God. One of these meaningful word pictures is that of the "door of hope," the open gate of grace for a repentant people. Let us explore this truth further as we consider the content of the text under the theme: The Door of Hope: (1) Man by his sins has brought himself into his present plight; (2) God in His grace opens the way of escape.

I

Man by His Sins Has Brought Himself into His Present Plight

Through the prophet Hosea God tells His people: Israel, thou hast destroyed thyself." You yourself

[46]

did it. The people brought themselves under God's displeasure chiefly by the sin of gross idolatry. In the Book of Hosea idolatry goes under the term "spiritual adultery." The picture is this: God, as Bridegroom and Husband, betrothed Himself to His people as His bride. There was sealed between them a covenant of love and faithfulness, as in holy wedlock. But Israel was not a faithful spouse. As frequently happens in human society, the spouse is not satisfied with her husband but seeks another. So Israel forsook the true God and took after the false god Baal. All this was to be poignantly dramatized in the marriage Hosea was instructed to consummate with Gomer, a woman of infidelity.

A loose woman, as is so often observed in our times also, will adhere to her friend as long as he promises good things: money, jewels, costly furs, delectable food and drink, and whatever else appeals to carnal appetites. By the same token, Israel in perpetration of spiritual adultery ran after Baal because it supposed: This god gives us corn, wine, oil, and multiplies my silver and gold. As on Thanksgiving Day and other occasions we thank God for the fruits of the land, so the Israelites thanked Baal at their feast days, new moons, Sabbaths, and solemn feasts.

That was dreadful idolatry, and God's anger was aroused. But we note, in Hosea's prophecy especially, that God's wrath is not separated from His love. What will He do in the anger of His affection? This is His resolve: I will take back My corn and wine, My wool and flax. I will destroy her vines and fig trees, because Israel regards them as Baal's gifts. I will hedge up her way with thorns and make a wall that she shall not find her paths.

[47]

That was a sore punishment, administered through the withdrawal of blessings. But always there is the gracious intent to regain a wayward people. It is as though a punishing father held the rod in one hand and the apple in the other. Israel, the spiritual harlot, shall come to know that these blessings, temporarily suspended, really came from God. God would have Israel resolve: "I will go and return to my first husband, for then was it better with me than now." Note how closely wrath and love work together, as they only can in the heart of God. This is demonstrated also in the text. God will deprive, but He will also allure and draw. He will bring Israel into the wilderness and He will speak comfortably to her.

When God withdraws His blessings and visits His people with much trouble, it is always time for them to pause and to ask: How did we get ourselves into this predicament? Is it not because of our idolatry? Did we not forget God and chase after other gods who promised us much earthly gain? These are questions that all the people of the world, especially Americans, should ask themselves in these precarious modern times.

Idolatry is still Sin Number One. "But," it will be interposed, "how is this possible? Baal worship has died out. In our times nobody speaks of this idol anymore." It is true: The god Baal is forgotten, but certainly idolatry, or the "worship" of false gods, is still with us. Fine idolatry is today Sin Number One, and so God continues to say in Commandment Number One: "Thou shalt have no other gods before Me."

Who are the gods served in our country? Are they not earthly things and earthly beings whom we fear, love, and trust more than God? There is the god Money, who goes by various aliases such as

Mammon, or Materialism. Oh, how people bow down before this would-be deity and say: You give us everything that is good and our hearts desire. Your gold and silver enable us to procure all that they can buy. Thank you! There is also the god Pleasure, who allures people and says: Your God is too holy, too serious; He deprives you of joy. Come with me, and I promise you enjoyment and pleasure. Here is wine, drink! Here is an inch-thick steak, eat! Here are companions who will celebrate with you during all of Saturday night, socialize with them! There is, further, the god You Yourself, and his near relative Man Himself. You Yourself, your arm, your wisdom, your own effort, and the science and technology of Man Himself give you everything. Love these gods, serve them, work for them!

So it has been in America, the land of plenty. Instead of thanking God and serving Him, many inhabitants have practiced fine idolatry. But it was not to go on indefinitely, for God has taken a hand in the situation in our day. God has unmistakably entered upon the scene of modern history, and He declares through the events of our time: "Twentieth-century man, you have turned your back on Me in your pursuit of wealth. Your 'American way of life' has been your god. Man, do you want to know something? Your gods have let you down. They have reduced you to your present desperate circumstances. You know this to be true now: In a minute's time everything can be taken from you. If but one mammoth thermonuclear device were to fall on your city or community, with the heat, force, and fury of nearly hell itself, nothing would remain."

Let us bear in mind, however, that the potential withdrawal of our blessings is not just a visitation but a divine measure to bring us back to God. Although man with his idolatry has gotten himself into the present plight and is in danger of total loss, the situation is not without God's gracious purpose. If our generation will repent, confess its idolatry, and begin the journey that leads back to God, the door of hope is open.

II

God's Grace Opens the Way of Escape

How does God prepare the way of escape? In our text we find one promise after another. The first of these is: "I will speak comfortably with her." Because Israel bethought herself of her ways and repented, God does not threaten anymore, does not reproach, but consoles. He will speak comfortably, as also He instructed Isaiah: "Comfort ye, comfort ye My people, saith your God."

The further assurance is given: "I will give her her vineyards from thence." Before, God spoke of destroying the vines and fig trees to bring Israel to her senses. Since the people made a spiritual about-face, it shall have the vineyards, the fact now being very clear that God gives them. In the valley of Achor, which was said to be a pleasant and fruitful valley, God opens the door of hope. The people shall reap, eat, live, and sing "as in the day when she came up out of the land of Egypt." This is a reference to Israel's deliverance from Pharaoh's charioteers at the time of the crossing of the Red Sea. Then the people, under the guidance of Moses and Miriam, encouraged one another: "Let us sing unto the Lord, for He has triumphed gloriously; the horse and his rider hath He thrown into the sea."

The Lord, as Opener of the door of hope, has His mind ever on reconciliation, for He is a forgiving God. He looks forward to reunion with His spouse, saying: "It shall be at that day . . . that thou shalt call Me 'My Husband,' and shalt call Me no more Baali," or "My Lord." Israel, as a faithless wife, had forsaken God. It had succumbed to the delusion that God could be served under the name of Baal. But she has confessed this error, and God is willing to accept her again. Let the spouse now address me as "My Husband," who loves Me and whom I love, and not as "My Baal," or master. Israel is not God's slave but His spouse. With this misunderstanding cleared up, let the name of Baal be forever erased, his memory blotted out, for the past is forgiven and forgotten.

Oh, how gracious is God in that He forgets and lets bygones be bygones! He says to every penitent and believing sinner: "We shall not speak of your past anymore." He makes no more accusations because past sins are forgiven. God has blotted out "the handwriting of ordinances that was against us, which was contrary to us, and took it out of the way, nailing it to His cross." The Law, with its written charges against us, was fulfilled, and so there is no longer a basis for accusing the believer of sin. Who has fulfilled all the demands of the Law and made restitution for our transgressions? It is Jesus Christ, who bare our sins in His own body on the tree. Through faith in Him we are forgiven, declared just, and reconciled. God Himself makes the declaration: Your sins are taken away. I have cast them behind Me. I have buried them in the depth of the sea, the way leaden containers with dangerous fall-out material are taken from atomic power plants and dumped into the depth of the ocean to be forever removed. The blood of Jesus Christ has cleansed you from all sin.

A further promise is stated in these words: "I will make a covenant for them with the beasts of the field,

[51]

and with the fowls of heaven, and with the creeping things of the ground." Many a crop was lost and often man went hungry because wild beasts, birds of prey, and grasshoppers ravaged fields and fruit trees. God reminds us here that also these creatures are in His hand, along with all forces of nature, whether floods, winds, or fires. "I will control them," God says, "so that they cannot cause you any more suffering."

Along the same lines, God has in His power all kings, princes, potentates, and world governments bent on making war. "I will break the bow and the sword and the battle out of the earth, and will make them to lie down in safety," He promises. The communist regimes of Russia and China, however war-minded they may be, cannot do what they want, for against them is the finger of God. They can go only so far and not one inch farther in their aggressions. History bears abundant witness of this. The Spaniards once sailed against England with their "invincible armada" to conquer it. What happened? God destroyed the fleet in a storm at sea. Napoleon, in another era, marched on Moscow, occupied it, and imagined that he had subjugated Russia. But when the Russians forced him out by burning Moscow, God stopped him, indeed not with a miracle of miracles or with a great catastrophe in nature, but with snow-flakes — with millions and millions of soft, gentle snowflakes.

Oh, the love of God which always opens the door of hope and prepares the way of salvation! His compassions fail not; they are new every morning; great is His faithfulness. This abiding faithfulness of God is the main burden of the message communicated by Hosea. It is stated and restated thus: "I will betroth thee unto Me forever; yea, I will betroth thee unto

Me in righteousness and in judgment and in loving-kindness and in mercies. I will even betroth thee unto Me in faithfulness, and thou shalt know the Lord."

The faithfulness of God is our hope in uncertain, dangerous times. As a zealous God He will indeed call to our minds the precarious situation our sins of idolatry have brought us into. In doing so, He does not leave us comfortless, or without hope. In mercy He opens the door of hope, draws us to Himself in the renewal of His covenant, and pledges mercy. By this love we are moved to return to Him and to trust firmly that "God is our Refuge and Strength, a very present Help in trouble."

JOEL

Everyone's Valley of Decision

Proclaim ye this among the Gentiles: Prepare war, wake up the mighty men, let all the men of war draw near; let them come up. Beat your plowshares into swords and your pruning hooks into spears. Let the weak say, I am strong. Assemble yourselves and come, all ye heathen, and gather yourselves together round about; thither cause Thy mighty ones to come down, O Lord. Let the heathen be wakened and come up to the valley of Jehoshaphat; for there will I sit to judge all the heathen round about. Put ye in the sickle, for the harvest is ripe. Come, get you down; for the press is full, the fats overflow; for their wickedness is great. Multitudes, multitudes in the Valley of Decision; for the Day of the Lord is near in the Valley of Decision. The sun and the moon shall be darkened, and the stars shall withdraw their shining. The Lord also shall roar out of Zion and utter His voice from Jerusalem; and the heavens and the earth shall shake; but the Lord will be the Hope of His people and the Strength of the children of Israel. So shall ye know that I am the Lord, your God, dwelling in Zion, My holy mountain. Then shall Jerusalem be holy, and there shall no strangers pass through her anymore. And it shall come to pass in that day that the mountains shall drop down new wine, and the hills shall flow with milk, and all the rivers of Judah shall flow with waters, and a fountain shall come forth of the house of the Lord.

Joel 3:9-18

Decisions! Decisions! This is an exclamation often heard. Life abounds with situations demanding that decisions be rendered for oneself and others. Shakespeare's "to be or not to be" is a question pressing for an answer. Similar problems are: to do or not to do, to go or not to go, to buy or not to buy. The responsibility increases when decisions involve the welfare of other people. Such is the case with questions facing fathers: "Where shall we establish homes for our families?" or "Is it safe to invest family savings in a new business?" Business executives, college presidents, army generals, city mayors, state governors, and others in positions of leadership must make far-reaching choices. They can understand what burden rests on the President of the United States as he, and he alone, must decide on courses of action affecting the lives of millions of fellow citizens.

It is not only in secular life that decisions must be made. Alternatives of greater import confront man in the spiritual realm, for not only temporal but eternal consequences are at stake. There is no escape from this encounter. While in other areas of life a sheltered, responsibility-dodging person may avoid making definite commitments, it is not possible to retreat from decisions on which man's relationship to God depends. This is a truth stated by the prophet Joel in a moving discourse which we may caption: Everyone's Valley of Decision: (1) God's summons to all people; (2) the time of grace is a time of decision; (3) the outcome of God's meeting with man.

I

God's Summons to All People

At the beginning of this chapter God expresses His awareness of His people held in captivity and scattered abroad in the world. It is His intention to gather them again. What is more, He will convene all nations for an accounting in the Valley of Jehoshaphat. The name is very likely symbolic, meaning "Jehovah has judged." Who is to assemble in this place of judgment? Named are Tyre and Zidon, all the coasts of Palestine, the Grecians, the Sabeans, in short, the Gentiles, the heathen. As for numbers, they are "multitudes, multitudes in the Valley of Decision."

Why this convocation of the nations? God has something important to say to them. They are to hear His plea in behalf of His people whom the Gentiles have abused. The nations are to know that it is God who reigns and that He will judge their actions. God's assembly call has the effect of rousing men from spiritual indifference to the realization that the halting between two opinions is no longer possible. It is time to face up to the crisis, to the great decision for or against the true God. Let all nations awaken to the urgency of the hour. The time of decision is here. The growing time, when judgments are kept in suspense because wheat and tares yet look alike, is now over. The harvest is ripe, revealing what has grown. It is time to put in the sickle and to make a determination of the yield.

When is the great day of the Lord in the Valley of Decision? Is it the final Judgment Day only, or does it include the preceding era, beginning with Pentecost Day, when the Gospel of the Kingdom is preached in the world as a witness against all nations? The text is indeed sprinkled with references to the Last Day. The context, however, indicates that the preceding period, namely, the time of the entire New Testament, is drawn in. The New Testament era is the "day of the Lord." It calls for decisions, and it culminates, of course, in the Final Judgment.

[56]

Let this not be confusing. It is not unusual for Biblical writers to combine topically events which, chronologically speaking, were widely separated by time. That is what Jesus Himself did when in His homilies on the last things He intertwined prophecies of the destruction of Jerusalem with prophecies of the end of the world. In doing this our Lord followed the example of the prophets. In the Book of Joel, for example, the great acts of God over long periods of time are telescoped into a single report. In one place Joel combines the outpouring of the Holy Spirit, which eventuated on Pentecost Day, with Judgment Day and the accompanying signs on sun and moon. He effects a similar blend of events in the text. The rallying of the nations in the Valley of Decision is merged with their final arraignment on the Last Day. The whole New Testament era in which the Gospel is proclaimed as a witness is here seen against the dramatic background of the final consummation. When are all men confronted by God for a decision or self-declaration? The time is now.

While the text addresses itself to nations in the aggregate, it is evident that in effect it speaks to individuals. Take away persons, and there are no nations. God's relationship is not only with people *en masse,* but also with individuals on an I-thou basis. His covenant with Israel was a covenant with individuals, with the circumcision of the individual as the outward mark. The multitude that John saw before God's throne in heaven is representative of the multitude even now summoned to the Valley of Decision. It breaks down into persons, the great and the small, the young and the old, and the like. Mankind arraigned before God at any given moment consists of persons. These persons are the lonely grandmother in yon house, the busy executive dashing from one

[57]

business appointment to another, the housewife hanging out wash, the young people preoccupied with plans for marriage and vocational careers, the student buried in books and reports, the beatnik, the conformist and the rugged individualist, the self-reliant man who supposedly needs no "religious crutch," the atheist, the humanist, the Christian. All are summoned into the divine presence to speak their yes or no to God's rule over their lives.

II

The Time of Grace Is a Time of Decision

The God of Judah and Jerusalem is a God who remembers mercy. He declares Himself to be "the Hope of His people and the Strength of the Children of Israel." In the time of the restoration, which will be consummated under the benign reign of the Messiah, divine grace will abound for all who have sinned. Joel has already prophesied of the time of grace, referring to the outpouring of the Holy Spirit without measure. By divine inspiration Peter declared this Messianic prophecy fulfilled in the events of Pentecost Day. What spiritual refreshment is not promised for the age of the Messiah and His Spirit! Not in measured drops, not in rivulets, but in abundant streams and with the opening of the windows of heaven is the Spirit given to revive an arid church. Here is the water of life at flood stage, for God promises: "I will pour out My Spirit upon all flesh, and your sons and your daughters shall prophesy, your old men shall dream dreams, your young men shall see visions." Lest there be any thought of the Lord restricting His grace, or withholding it from people of low estate, He adds, "And also upon the servants and upon the handmaids in those days will I pour out My Spirit."

[58]

The abundance of grace in the day of the Lord's Anointed is vividly depicted also in these words: "The mountains shall drop down new wine, and the hills shall flow with milk, and all the rivers of Judah shall flow with waters, and a fountain shall come forth of the house of the Lord." Wine, milk, water — these are the symbols of God's grace, full and free. Isaiah extends the invitation to all in Israel and other nations to partake of this grace, saying: "Ho, everyone that thirsteth, come ye to the waters, and he that hath no money, come ye, buy and eat; yea, come, buy wine and milk without money and without price."

The time of spiritual abundance was ushered in when our Lord Jesus Christ, as the Messiah of whom Moses and the Prophets testified, began His ministry. He referred to Himself as Food and Drink for the soul, as the Bread come down from heaven, and the living Water. St. John pronounced the incarnate Word as "full of grace and truth," adding, "Of His fullness have all we received, and grace for grace." The abundance of God's grace in Christ becomes so evident when it is compared with man's spiritual poverty. As though two things were weighed against each other, the one far outstrips the other, for where sin abounded, grace did much more abound. What is more, the riches of divine grace are intended to save man from the poverty of sin, as Paul writes: "For ye know the grace of our Lord Jesus Christ, that though He was rich, yet for your sakes He became poor, that ye through His poverty might become rich."

In complete renunciation of His own life our Lord entered death itself to enrich us with forgiveness of sins, life, and salvation. These are the riches of His grace. This is the wine, milk, and water for the soul. Christ imparts these blessings through the Word and the sacraments, that God's people may be abundantly

[59]

satisfied with the fatness of His house and drink of the river of His pleasures.

Salvation and all its blessing are still being offered to all mankind in this time of grace. "Come, accept My love," is God's invitation to all. The blessings of divine grace cannot, however, be spurned with impunity. They cannot be ignored as though they had not been proffered. The time of grace is the time of decision. Now that Christ has come, there can be no indifference, no lukewarmness. Man in the valley of decision must declare himself as either for or against Him. Christ is the great catalyst. In aged Simeon's words, He is "set for the fall and rising again of many in Israel." For some He is the Rock of Ages and for others, in Peter's statement, "a stone of stumbling and a rock of offense."

Christ's grace summons everyone into the Valley of Decision, either to gather with Him or to scatter, to be disciple or destroyer, friend or foe. Now is the time to make up one's mind. Now is the hour to stand on His side and resolve with Joshua: "As for me and my house, we will serve the Lord." This is a pledge that people who are already believers can and should renew. Those who are unconverted still cannot, of course, make any such decision for God. The call to repentance is nevertheless addressed to them, because it occurs always in and with the proclamation of the Gospel, through which the Holy Spirit gives new hearts, minds, and wills.

III

The Outcome of God's Meeting with Man

God convenes the nations in the Valley of Decision. Meetings among human beings are sometimes convened and then adjourned without definite, fruit-

ful outcomes. God's meetings with man are not of
that kind. When He assembles all mankind for an
important confrontation, there are results, for His
Spirit is at work in human hearts. What are the results? They are not uniformly the same in all hearers.
Some people answer the divine summons in a spirit
of hostility, bringing the weapons of spiritual warfare.
In some the hatred of God will be intensified, and
they will forge weapons for attacks. In others, however, the spiritual warfare against God will end.
These former warriors, when they perceive God's
thoughts of peace toward them, will in a reversal of
terms beat their swords into plowshares and their
spears into pruning hooks. Like Saul the Pharisee,
a once mighty warrior against Christ, they will be
converted and will henceforth devote all their energy
to the upbuilding of Christ's peaceable kingdom.

The meeting in the Valley of Decision, to use another picture, will result in a harvest of souls for
eternity. Again, not all will want to be sheaves gar-
nered into heaven's granary. The time of crisis will
show the difference between the wheat and the tares,
and some will prefer to remain tares. However, there
will also be a good harvest when the Lord puts in
His sickle. John the Baptist proclaimed the time of
testing and its outcome thus: "He will thoroughly
purge His floor and gather His wheat into the gar-
ner. . . ." In the footsteps of John came Jesus, who
also visualized the time of the harvest. He saw the
fields white to harvest. He called for laborers to be
sent into the harvest of world missions. The sifting
process that goes on whenever and wherever the Gospel is preached as a witness is now, and the firstfruits
are evident now. Its outcome foreshadows the final
disposition on Judgment Day, when "the angels shall
come forth and sever the wicked from among the just."

[61]

At all events, whether the outcome is acceptance or rejection of salvation, all men shall know, as God expresses it through Joel: "that I am the Lord, your God, dwelling in Zion." Even the wicked, who are lost by their decision against God and His Anointed, must acknowledge the sovereignty of God. So much better it is when the knowledge of God is accompanied by confidence in Him. Then knowing God is a matter not only of the head but also of the heart. It is then the saving knowledge of God, as our Lord did say: "This is life eternal, that they might know Thee, the only true God, and Jesus Christ, whom Thou hast sent."

Everyone is summoned by God into the Valley of Decision. Grace is offered, but grace that presses for man's acceptance of it. The time of grace is thus entitled: "Behold, now is the accepted time; behold, now is the day of salvation." The desired outcome of God's meeting with man is always what Isaiah recorded: "In an acceptable time have I heard thee, and in a day of salvation have I helped thee; and I will preserve thee and give thee for a covenant of the people, to establish the earth, to cause to inherit the desolate heritages." May God's summons always find us saying with Samuel: "Speak, Lord, for Thy servant heareth."

AMOS

The Plumb Line in God's Hand

Thus he showed me, and behold, the Lord stood upon a wall made by a plumb line, with a plumb line in His hand. And the Lord said unto me, Amos, what seest thou? And I said, A plumb line. Then said the Lord, Behold, I will set a plumb line in the midst of My people Israel; I will not again pass by them anymore. And the high places of Isaac shall be desolate, and the sanctuaries of Israel shall be laid waste; and I will rise against the house of Jeroboam with the sword.

Amos 7:7-9

In that day will I raise up the tabernacle of David that is fallen, and close up the breaches thereof; and I will raise up his ruins, and I will build it as in the days of old, that they may possess the remnant of Edom, and of all the heathen which are called by My name, saith the Lord that doeth this. Behold, the days come, saith the Lord, that the plowman shall overtake the reaper, and the treader of grapes him that soweth seed; and the mountains shall drop sweet wine, and all the hills shall melt. And I will bring again the captivity of My people of Israel, and they shall build the waste cities and inhabit them; and they shall plant vineyards and drink the wine thereof; they shall also make gardens and eat the fruit of them. And I will plant them upon their land, and they shall no more be pulled up out of their land which I have given them, saith the Lord, thy God.

Amos 9:11-15

---

[63]

IT CAN BE SAID that God originated the use of visual-aid materials. In the Book of Amos we are told how God showed a series of visions to the prophet. In these visions He caused Amos to see various meaningful objects. As a good teacher, God had the prophet concentrate on the visualized objects and repeat what he saw. These visions, because they contained deep moral and spiritual lessons, were more than illustrations; they were parables in picture form. From the things seen applications were to be made to the spiritual state of the people of Israel.

So very plain were the objects shown to Amos that artists could readily paint a series of pictures of them and entitle them according to their identification in the text, namely, "Grasshoppers," "The Devouring Fire," "A Basket of Summer Fruit," "The Plumb Line," and "The Altar in Bethel." In fact, we know of an artist, F. W. Thomsen, who made an abstract sketch of the plumb line. The magazine *Response* described the picture as follows:

"Eternal order and truth have always existed within the erratic and thorny pattern of history. Often conflicting forces fill all space, threatening to destroy the inheritance that God has given to us. In spite of the conflict there are reminders of the eternal: the sea with its waves constantly washing the shore, changing granite boulders into golden sand; the horizon that is always level, and the perpendicular force of gravity. These and the eternal love of God are constants within the changing pattern of time."

Since Amos' vision of the plumb line has such significance for our time, let us give closer attention to it now. The Plumb Line in God's Hand: (1) It is extended in judgment on the house of Israel and its false sanctuaries; (2) it is extended for the upbuilding of the tabernacle of David.

[64]

I

It Is Extended in Judgment on the House of Israel and Its False Sanctuaries

Amos prophesied against iniquities rampant in the Northern Kingdom. Because his testimony was sharp, it was resented. There was tolerance for the prophet as long as he directed his criticisms to neighboring nations, such as Egypt, Edom, Syria, or the southern kingdom of Judah. When he turned his attention to Israel, there was objection. Amaziah, the priest of Bethel, told him: "O thou seer, go, flee thee away into the land of Judah, and there eat bread, and prophesy there. But prophesy not again anymore at Bethel; for it is the king's chapel, and it is the king's court." A modern version of this objection is found in the fourth stanza of Charlotte Perkins Gilman's poem *To the Preacher:*

> Preach about the other man, Preacher!
>   The man we all can see!
> The man of oaths, the man of strife,
> The man who drinks and beats his wife,
> Who helps his mates to fret and shirk
> When all they need is to keep at work —
> Preach about the other man, Preacher!
>   Not about me!

In reply, Amos stoutly defended his divine call to prophesy in Israel, reminding Amaziah: "I was an herdman and a gatherer of sycamore fruit. And the Lord took me as I followed the flock, and the Lord said unto me, Go, prophesy unto My people Israel." He was not about to be cowed into silence. His answer to veiled threats was: "Now therefore hear thou the Word of the Lord."

What sins of Israel did Amos castigate? What was amiss in the kingdom? In relation to God, the people led by king and priests sinned with their idolatry. The seat of idolatrous worship was Bethel, where the royal palace and the sanctuary were located. In Bethel, Jeroboam I had erected a golden calf to paganize the religion of Israel. The present king, Jeroboam II, continued this center of idolatry. Wild orgies marked the festive activities of the sanctuary, as Amos charges: "They lay themselves down upon clothes laid to pledge by every altar, and they drink the wine of the condemned in the house of their god." Particularly wicked were the efforts, by temptation and threat, to profane people who had taken solemn vows. According to Amos, they "gave the Nazarites wine to drink, and commanded the prophets, saying, Prophesy not."

True religion was corrupted not only by the admixture of heathen rites but also by the reduction of worship to sterile, perfunctory rendition. God said to all this: "I hate, I despise your feast days, and I will not smell in your solemn assemblies. Though ye offer Me burnt offerings and your meat offerings, I will not accept them, neither will I regard the peace offerings of your fat beasts." Giving further impetus to the profanation of religion was the craven professionalism of the priests, with Amaziah as their chief. A thorn in the side of the carnally secure priests were the prophets, such as Amos, whose mind was not on pleasing men but on obeying God.

When man's relation to God is distorted and shown to be so in perverted religious worship, it is but a short step to the perversion of man's relation to fellowman. In Israel moral conditions sank to a low state. With the right relation to God ruptured, the doors were opened to moral decline. There was

[66]

nothing to restrain man from going beyond and defrauding his brother. There was no buffer for the impact of a changing economy that victimized the many dispossessed "little people."

At this time society in Israel changed from simple agrarianism to more complex agricultural and commercial enterprises. Amos was most reluctant to see feudal landlords amassing small farms, for it meant dispossessing families and reducing free men to serfs. There are shades here of the Steinbeck novel *The Grapes of Wrath*, only the shades were darker. To this extent were the poor the pawns of the rich: "They sold the righteous for silver, and the poor for a pair of shoes." How incensed was Amos with idle patricians lolling in mischievous leisure and luxury! He knew what went on at their wild parties as they lay on their ivory beds and stretched themselves on their couches at the banquet tables. They corrupted good manners and the fine arts as they chanted "to the sound of the viol" in the hoarse voices of drunkenness.

Because Amos protested social injustices, some have tried to make him out the "father of the social gospel." But Amos is far more than a shallow social reformer. He speaks as a man of God. Never does he detach man's relation to man from his prior relation to God. Social sins, Amos insists, are sins against the Lord, in that they are transgressions of God's holy Law. The way to correct social wrongs is to apply to offenders, in their proper order, the Word of the Law and the Word of promise. This is what Amos did in his repeated "Hear this Word!"

Through the testimony of His prophets God lowers the plumb line in the midst of His people to reveal its moral and spiritual crookedness. The third in Amos' series of five visions is that of the Lord standing "upon a wall made by a plumb line, with a plumb line in His hand." The Lord inquires: "Amos, what seest thou?" The prophet replies: "A plumb line." There follows the meaning of the plumb line: "Behold, I will set a plumb line in the midst of My people Israel; I will not again pass by them anymore." The Lord has come to make an exact measurement and to punish king, priests, and people for their moral aberrations. This He threatens: "The high places of Isaac shall be desolate, and the sanctuaries of Israel shall be laid waste; and I will rise against the house of Jeroboam with the sword."

The plumb line in God's hand represents the truth that God is not given to casual whims but to invariable principles of justice. As an exact mathematician He insists that two times two is four and not five. As an exact moral physicist He cannot be satisfied with claims that water freezes at indeterminate temperature readings. God's plumb line yields exact data. He who holds it in his hand is a God of rectitude and of Moral Law. He calls to account and to judgment all who depart from His rule.

Amos' vision of the plumb line teaches that the Moral Law of God is straight. The Law of God is a rule, norm, standard, or criterion. It shows sinful man his departure from the specifications of divine righteousness. If as spiritual masons or bricklayers men have built a crooked wall, the plummet hanging perpendicularly from above — from God's own hand — will show it. The Law of God is a rule also for those who in faith seek to do good works. While it cannot motivate right living and right doing (for only faith in the Gospel can do this), it can serve as a guide. In Ps. 119 the question is asked: "Wherewithal shall a young man cleanse his way?" The reply is given: "By taking heed thereto according to Thy

Word." Likewise, St. Paul writes: "All Scripture is given by inspiration of God and is profitable for doctrine, for reproof, for correction, for instruction in righteousness, that the man of God may be perfect, thoroughly furnished unto all good works."

Thank God for the plumb line! It is absolutely true and reliable. It does not curve, bend, or vary to suit man's fancies. Human opinions, as well as moral regulations based on such quicksand, are apt to be affected by changing conditions and thus become relative. They are therefore a very inadequate guide for moral behavior. One generation may consider it wrong to steal, another that it is wrong only to steal from friends, another that it is wrong to steal from private persons but not from public institutions or corporations. But God's Law will not budge to accommodate changing opinions. It is an umpire whose decisions are given with fairness and finality, without fear or favor. It is a judge of the hearts, handing down just verdicts.

As a people under the rule of God we must acknowledge the rightness and propriety of the divine plumb line in human affairs. All human affairs are God's affairs. For us it is never a question when actions or nonactions are contemplated: "Is it profitable?" or "Is it expedient?" or "Is it popular?" Always the question is: "Is it right according to the perfect Law of God?" This perfect Law tells us in its two major pronouncements to love God fully and to love the neighbor fully. These are clear, timeless, eternal principles. Church and society do the right thing when they make determination of all problems in the clear light of these mandates. The failure to do so brings down God's plumb line for judgment, as at the time of apostasy in Israel.

[69]

II

It Is Extended for the Upbuilding of the Tabernacle of David

In the vision God appeared standing on a wall, as if to measure the sinful house of Israel and its false sanctuaries. In the closing chapter we read of God's purpose with regard to another structure, namely, the tabernacle of David. In rebuilding the latter the Lord again holds a plumb line in His hand, not for judgment but for a constructive reason. The plumb line is now an instrument for right building, for the edification of His spiritual temple. The tabernacle of David, which has fallen to ruins, is to be reconstructed and the holes in the walls repaired. Although much of it now lies waste, the foundations are still there. The whole edifice can and will be restored to its former beauty. In fact, it will be erected on a much grander scale.

What is meant by the tabernacle of David? Who is David? We always keep in mind that at this time King David was long deceased. References in prophetic writings to "David," to "My Servant David," or a Davidic Shepherd, as Isaiah, Jeremiah, Ezekiel, and Hosea make such references, are to the Messiah, who is both David's Son and David's Lord. The tabernacle of David is thus the New Testament church under Jesus Christ, the Messiah.

The spiritual tool for the upbuilding of the Christian church is not the Mosaic Law but the Gospel. Amos in chapter nine is the voice of God proclaiming the Word of promise. As in previous chapters he applied the Law in all its exactitude, so now he declares the goodness of God in the Gospel. This sweet and comforting message is addressed to Israelites as well as "the remnant of Edom and of all the heathen which are called" by the Lord's name.

The Law and the Gospel are here, as in other Biblical settings, presented in their seeming tension, or contradiction. Here is a problem puzzling many people. They ask, "How can God be just and at the same time merciful? How can He condemn and then forgive?" This will be a real difficulty, unless one understands the relationship of the Law and the Gospel. Some, who are not aware of this relationship, try to solve the problem by saying that God tempers justice with mercy, that in love He simply overrules His righteousness. This, of course, a righteous God cannot do. He cannot yield one iota of His justice. Neither will it do to say that God is constantly changing His mind or His mood. He would not be a God worthy of the name or of man's respect if He were so fickle in His emotions as to demand obedience in one breath and in the next pronounce forgiveness of man's disobedience.

The only bridge from the justice to the grace of God is the Mediator Jesus Christ. As man's Substitute, Jesus Christ rendered perfect obedience to God's Law. Of Him God demanded fulfillment. Of Him, as the Lamb of God, He exacted the full penalty for man's transgressions. Jesus rendered full satisfaction in the sight of the just God for all mankind's iniquity. He did this when He was set forth an offering on the cross of Calvary.

God now applies the plumb line to all who accept the Savior in faith and finds them perfect. He measures them, not with their own righteousness, but with the righteousness of Christ, declaring them just. It may be asked, "If God is satisfied because in Christ equals have been rendered for equals, where does

God's forgiving love come in?" This is His love, namely, that He so fervently cared for sinners that He gave His only-begotten Son. It is the utmost love, a love prompting the supreme sacrifice, a love that in Christ forgives penitent and believing man all his sins.

The Gospel is the Good News of the love of God in Christ Jesus. It announces and conveys to believers the perfect righteousness of Christ. It is the new plumb line, building tool, and divine means utilized by the Holy Spirit for the upbuilding of God's spiritual temple. You who have been brought to faith in the Son of God are become lively stones in the structure of the holy Christian church, the communion of saints. You represent one more step toward the completion of the tabernacle of David in the time foreseen by Amos.

It is the divine offer of grace and forgiveness that God would have us proclaim to the world, to the Israelites, Ethiopians, Philistines, Syrians, and all other people of our time. They are all to be included in the tabernacle of David. The mission of the church is to let down the plumb line of the Gospel, to preach that God was in Christ, reconciling the world unto Himself. It is only through the proclamation of the Word of reconciliation that the tabernacle of David can be raised up, built out, and enlarged throughout all ages.

The promise of blessings on the church in the day of the Messiah is set forth in poetic terms, such as these: "The mountains shall drop sweet wine, and all the hills shall melt." Again, God's people "shall plant vineyards and drink the wine thereof; they shall also make gardens and eat the fruit of them." Projected here is the picture of the fruitfulness of the New Testament church, with God pleased to have men as His co-workers. The vineyard of the church is indeed His workmanship, for He declares: "I will raise up" and "I will build it." Referring to the members of spiritual Israel, He says: "I will plant them upon their land." At the same time He expects the members to build and plant. In fact, He enlists them for service in His kingdom, saying: "They shall plant vineyards . . . they shall also make gardens."

Amos in a vision saw the Lord with a plumb line in His hand. It is given us to see this plumb line in the written Word of God. This plummet is the Law of God pronouncing on evildoers the judgment that the wages of sin is death. It is also, in a climactic sense, the Gospel, announcing that the gift of God is eternal life through Jesus Christ. For the Christian the plumb line of judgment is taken away, being replaced by the plumb line of the righteousness of Christ. Be comforted, then, as you hear also St. Paul assure you: "Who shall lay anything to the charge of God's elect? It is God that justifieth. Who is he that condemneth? It is Christ that died, yea rather, that is risen again, who is even at the right hand of God, who also maketh intercession for us."

OBADIAH

A Nest Among the Stars

Thus saith the Lord God concerning Edom: We have heard a rumor from the Lord, and an ambassador is sent among the heathen, Arise ye, and let us rise up against her in battle. Behold, I have made thee small among the heathen; thou art greatly despised. The pride of thine heart hath deceived thee, thou that dwellest in the clefts of the rock, whose habitation is high; that saith in his heart, Who shall bring me down to the ground? Though thou exalt thyself as the eagle, and though thou set thy nest among the stars, thence will I bring thee down, saith the Lord.

Obadiah 1-4

IN THE SPACE AGE scientific man is able to reach farther out into the universe. He can put various vehicles into orbit. The time may not be far off when he can gain a firmer foothold in space by launching a platform and anchoring it among the planets. Much of what is learned from space explorations is useful for life. As in another age mankind benefited from extensive sea voyages, so it can profit again from space travel. To a Christian the heavens declare the glory of God. Abraham Lincoln once said, "I cannot conceive how a man could look up into the heavens and say there is no God." If to a Christian a partial, human-eye view of celestial bodies already inspired admiration for the Creator, how much more should not a more thorough knowledge of the universe incite him to the praise of God!

For a people that denies the existence of God, space explorations will not have this effect. Moreover, such efforts are apt to become projects of human pride or events planned in celebration of man's genius. The builders of the Tower of Babel were motivated by sinful pride when they proposed to enter space by way of a spired skyscraper. Also today man's determination to settle the moon and establish outposts on even more remote planets can be a reenactment of the sin of ancient Edom. It is to the latter that Obadiah addresses his remonstrating message, charging them with setting A Nest Among the Stars: (1) The practice of pride; (2) the price of pride; (3) the purification of pride.

I

The Practice of Pride

The prophecy of Obadiah in these verses is directed against Edom, a people occupying the mountain fastnesses to the south of the Dead Sea. As descendants of Esau, the Edomites ought to have felt like blood brothers to the Israelites, who were the descendants of Jacob. Instead, the old enmity between Esau and Jacob filtered down through many generations. The people of Edom, in their hostility, were opportunists. When a powerful invader, probably the Chaldeans, attacked the land of Judah, the Edomites took sides against their brothers. Obadiah refers to the "violence against thy brother Jacob" and to the day when "thou stoodest on the other side."

Edom, because of its imagined impregnable position in the clefts of the rocks, was proud. The prophet

[75]

declares: "The pride of thine heart hath deceived thee." There was even then "Maginot Line" thinking, as referred to thus: "That saith in his heart, Who shall bring me down to the ground?" High up in the mountaintops the Edomites took their place, like eagles building their nests on inaccessible heights. "Though thou exaltest thyself as the eagle, and though thou set thy nest among the stars, thence will I bring thee down, saith the Lord," according to Obadiah.

The practice of pride detailed in the text is a carbon copy of overconfidences befalling other nations, past and present. National pride easily attaches itself to fortresses, armies, navies, air forces, and the weapons with which these are supplied. What is not always realized is the rapid rate of obsolescence. A strong bastion of former years may be weak today. The Chinese Wall was not for always to keep out invading hordes. The guns of Singapore in World War II were obsolete. The enemy did not come by water, as was anticipated, but by air across rice paddies. The heavy guns pointing out to sea could not be turned around to fire on attacking planes. Our country, too, with its supposedly unconquerable Corregidor in the Philippines, felt the sting of misplaced confidence.

This is therefore a statement right on target: "The pride of thine heart hath deceived thee." It is the nature of pride to deceive, both nations and individuals. Many are the times when proud people regard their position, prestige, wealth, or wisdom a hedge against misfortunes. The rich farmer of Christ's parable, whose servants brought in another bumper crop, looked to full granaries for his security. Our Lord quoted him as saying: "Soul, thou hast much goods laid up for many years; take thine ease, eat, drink, and be merry." Whatever else may be said of this attitude, marked as it was by materialism and short-sightedness, pride was an important element in it. No word was said about the providence and love of God. It was the man himself, *his* ground, *his* ingenuity, *his* diligence that received the credit. But how deceptive such pride! It left so many facts out of consideration, among them the insecurity of wealth, what with thieves, moths, rust, and the corrosive powers of inflation always working to reduce a man's possessions. What is more, no account was taken of human mortality. Death can so quickly step in to cut short a prosperous career and to deprive the individual of the enjoyment of his accumulated wealth.

Pride is always deceptive, because it leads a person to make unwarranted assumptions about himself and his things. The devil and his angels were deceived in their pride when they presumed to be above their Creator and could with immunity disobey Him. Man, too, is often deceived. With insufferable pride King Pharaoh of Egypt said to Moses and Aaron: "Who is the Lord that I should obey His voice?" He was to find out later his utter subjection to the true God. Roman emperors, frail human beings that they were, suffered from the delusion of pride when they called themselves divine. It is pride, again without foundation, that prompts the Antichrist to sit in the temple of God, pretending to be God. There is nothing at all to support these boasts, as little as there is truth in the claim of poor, deluded patients in mental hospitals who call themselves Alexander the Great or Napoleon.

When the Bible concludes all people under sin, it charges them all with sinful pride, with the ambition of wanting to set their nests among the stars. The psalmist's prayer is one all Christians pray after him: "Keep back Thy servant also from presumptuous

sins." In self-estimates one ought never to go beyond
the bounds of truth, for then there is danger of falling
into the trap of pride. This is St. Paul's counsel to us:
"I say, through the grace given unto me, to every
man that is among you, not to think of himself more
highly than he ought to think."

Pride walks among us today, now in disguise, now
in unabashed openness under well-known symbols.
Vance Packard, the author of *The Hidden Persuaders*,
finds many people "caught up in a relentless pursuit
of the emblems of status and success." A materially-
minded nation lays great store by such status markers
as furs, jewels, suburban villas, exclusive country
club memberships, and prestige charity committees.
Christians whom God has blessed with this world's
goods do not let wealth and its accompanying honor
go to their heads. They, like Abraham, are humble
in their prosperity. The problem lies mostly with
those who are pressing, who are engaged in a relentless effort to keep up with the Joneses, and indeed
not the Joneses of their class but those of a higher
bracket. The temptation is great to become presumptuous, to put on airs, to assume proud stances when
there is no basis for them.

II

The Price of Pride

Edom in its pride and false sense of security had
asked: "Who shall bring me down to the ground?"
To that question the Lord replied through Obadiah:
"I will bring thee down." The Edomites, who had
helped sack Jerusalem and spoke "proudly in the day
of distress," were to pay the price of their presumptuous acts. They were to be repaid in the same coin:
"As thou hast done, it shall be done unto thee." The

penalty was great, for its wise men were destroyed, its mighty men dismayed, its people cut off. Its allies turned out to be ungrateful friends, for "they that eat thy bread have laid a wound under thee." In a sentence, the price of pride may be computed thus: "I have made thee small among the heathen; thou art greatly despised." The aerie that Edom had set among the stars came tumbling down.

Sin always claims its wages. The sin of pride, too, has its price. The haughty empires of the past lie in dust. With many the decline and final demise came because in pride they overreached themselves. Nineveh, Babylon, Carthage, Troy, and other capital cities are no more. Nineveh in the days of Nahum was a world-famous commercial center, having multiplied its merchants, in Nahum's words, "above the stars of heaven." It was also a "bloody city," not at all hesitant to build material prosperity on slave labor and the subjection of other peoples. Nations with a "master race" complex always do this without moral scruples. Nineveh was long ago carried to its grave, an urban grave that is today of interest only to antiquarians.

Pride exacts its price also from individuals. It would be hard to imagine a person more proud than King Nebuchadnezzar of Babylon, who, among other acts of arrogance, had a golden image made and commanded his subjects to worship it. As a punishment for his many deeds of pride, Nebuchadnezzar, as Daniel relates, "was driven from men and did eat grass as oxen, and his body was wet with the dew of heaven, till his hairs were grown like eagles' feathers, and his nails like birds' claws." God has His ways of resisting haughty spirits, of abasing those who exalt themselves, of scattering the proud in the imagination of their hearts.

[79]

The "pride of life," which St. John identifies as a mark of the world, makes itself felt in our society with price tags showing. It has many aspects, many expressions. One of them is certainly pride of race and, by the same token, indifference if not contempt toward minority groups. In a moral world which God rules, the future will not be on the side of people claiming racial superiority. Always it is true: God resists the proud, but gives grace to the humble.

On workday mornings two groups of metropolitan people meet, the one group coming in and the other going out. Entering the city in commuter trains or other modes of transportation are the suburbanites, mostly business and professional people, reading their copies of the *Wall Street Journal.* Heading in the opposite directions are maids and servants from the inner city to do their menial jobs in suburban homes. One often sees them reading their Bibles. There is something disquieting about all this.

It is, of course, not wrong for anyone to live in the suburbs, to follow a business or professional career in the city, and to read helpful news journals en route. Neither is manual labor as done by the other group in any wise a disgrace. What is worth considering here is whether 20th-century man is putting himself on the side of God. If he does, God will be on his side. God is no respecter of the *status quo.* Those who love His Word, however lowly their present estate, He will exalt. What of the proud? What of those who "have" because they took it from others or refused to share? The Lord has His ways with them too. This is sure: Any social order built on social injustice will not endure. The time will come, perhaps sooner than expected, when pride, snobbery, discrimination, and other sins of man against man will demand their price.

[80]

III

The Purification of Pride

In the feud between Edom and Israel God had the last word. Obadiah makes this clear in the final sentence, which is a key statement: "The kingdom shall be the Lord's." The final victory will not be Israel's but God's. The holy seer anticipates the time when God will set His King on the holy hill of Zion. This King, as clearly stated in Ps. 2, is God's Son, the Anointed. Beyond the immediate historical situation with its political overtones, the prophet visualizes spiritual redemption, for the kingdom shall be the Lord's. He writes: "Upon Mount Zion shall be deliverance, and there shall be holiness." This is the purification of pride.

Not only for Edomites but also for Israelites shall there be a purification, for "the house of Jacob shall be a fire, and the house of Joseph a flame." Purification from sin is a keynote sounded by other of Obadiah's prophetic colleagues. "I will turn My hand upon thee and purely purge away thy dross and take away all thy tin," God announces through Isaiah. Malachi sees the Messiah "as a refiner and purifier of silver; and He shall purify the sons of Levi and purge them as gold and silver, that they may offer unto the Lord an offering in righteousness." "Then," as he continues, "shall the offering of Judah and Jerusalem be pleasant unto the Lord, as in the days of old."

Jesus Christ as the Messiah purified His people from their sins. The author of Hebrews states: "Who being the brightness of His glory, and the express image of His person, and upholding all things by the word of His power, when He had Himself purged our sins, sat down on the right hand of the Majesty

[81]

on high." How did He purge our sins? St. John puts it succinctly: "The blood of Jesus Christ, His Son, cleanseth us from all sin." Christ brought an offering of righteousness pleasant unto the Lord. In all things man's Substitute, He by His great humility atoned for all our sins, including the sin of pride. He humbled Himself and became obedient unto death, even the death of the cross.

How wonderful the power that cleanses man of pride! The purifying, pride-destroying power of Christ is seen at work in the hearts of His own. Saul of Tarsus was once a proud Pharisee. After he was converted to the Christian faith, he, as Paul the apostle, was a humble servant, counting all things but loss that he might gain Christ. From him we are gladly instructed to let that mind dwell in us which was also in Christ Jesus.

Purified of sinful pride, Christ's people adorn themselves with His humility and modesty. Now they are able to see themselves in the right light. Not at all alien to the virtue of humility but very much a part of it is proper self-esteem. Self-esteem means to have proper regard for oneself as a person whom God the Father has created, God the Son has redeemed, and God the Holy Ghost has sanctified. A Christian cannot think cheaply of himself, for Christ has paid a dear price for his redemption. True humility always issues in becoming self-respect and in thankfulness to God, because by His grace we are what we are.

God will not be a party to man's individual or corporate ambition to set his nest among the stars. In His mercy He has a much better plan to unfold for man's exaltation, and that is to lead him on the path of the Christian faith to human dignity and self-realization, to noble achievements in Christian service, and finally to the heavenly home on high. These goals God fulfills in us always by grace, not of works, lest any man should boast. Should we at all look up to the stars? Indeed we should. In the upward look of faith we behold Christ, our Polestar. As Christ ascended up far above all heavens that He might fill all things, so would He draw us to Himself, that where He is we may be also.

JONAH

Righting a Wrong-Way Missionary

Now the word of the Lord came unto Jonah, the son of Amittai, saying, Arise, go to Nineveh, that great city, and cry out against it; for their wickedness is come up before Me. But Jonah rose up to flee unto Tarshish from the presence of the Lord, and went down to Joppa; and he found a ship going to Tarshish; so he paid the fare thereof and went down into it, to go with them unto Tarshish from the presence of the Lord.

Jonah 1:1-3

And God saw their works, that they turned from their evil way; and God repented of the evil that He had said that He would do unto them; and He did it not. But it displeased Jonah exceedingly, and he was very angry. And he prayed unto the Lord and said, I pray Thee, O Lord, was not this my saying when I was yet in my country? Therefore I fled before unto Tarshish; for I knew that Thou art a gracious God and merciful, slow to anger and of great kindness, and repentest Thee of the evil. Therefore now, O Lord, take, I beseech Thee, my life from me; for it is better for me to die than to live.

Jonah 3:10—4:3

IT WAS NOT ONLY IN APOSTOLIC but also in prophetic times that God sent out missionaries. The ministries of several Old Testament prophets had a definite missionary aspect. Isaiah readily volunteered to be a home missionary in Jerusalem, responding to the

[84]

divine call with "Here am I, send me." While he himself, as far as we know, did not go to foreign lands, he was vitally concerned about the conversion of the heathen. He prophesied: "The Gentiles shall come to Thy light, and kings to the brightness of Thy rising." Amos likewise was obedient to his divine commission to cross the border of the Southern Kingdom and to bear witness in the Kingdom of Israel.

What is more, God in the time of old sent prophets to make direct contact with heathen people. Elijah resided in the home of a woman in Zarephath, and Elisha was in touch with Naaman the Syrian. Of the literary prophets, Jonah was a foreign missionary sent to preach the Word of God to the Gentiles in Nineveh.

Jonah, at first reluctant to venture into enemy territory, eventually did go on his mission. Arriving in Nineveh, he was, however, of a wrong attitude still, for he objected to God's resolve to save the penitent Ninevites. There was much that Jonah had to overcome before he became an instrument for good in God's hands. Jonah by and by learned his lesson well and did become an effective worker in a foreign field. This is the subject we intend to discuss as we present: Righting a Wrong-Way Missionary: (1) Jonah became a missionary when he returned from his flight and preached the Word in Nineveh; (2) Jonah became a missionary when he understood that God would rather save than destroy sinners.

I

Jonah Became a Missionary When He Returned from His Flight and Preached the Word in Nineveh

A generation ago an American aviator captured newspaper headlines when he made a surprise flight to Europe instead of going to the West Coast, as was

[85]

seemingly his plan. He told authorities that by mistake he flew east instead of west, and was promptly nicknamed "Wrong Way" Corrigan. Jonah gave a similar performance when he fled west instead of going east to preach the Word in Nineveh. This was not a mistake on his part. The missionary designate, for reasons of his own, disobeyed God and chose an opposite course.

The Bible records instances of men who initially were unwilling to undertake difficult missions but then were persuaded to go. Moses was at first most reluctant to appear before Pharaoh and confront him with the divine mandate to let Israel go. Eventually he was prevailed upon to carry out his assignment. To Jeremiah God said: "I ordained thee a prophet unto the nations." The prophet pleaded his youthfulness as a reason for being excused. He said: "Ah, Lord God, behold, I cannot speak, for I am a child." His hesitancy, however, was not disobedience. When the Lord touched his mouth, he consented to the mission. Moses and Jeremiah were not unlike the son in Jesus' parable to whom the father said, "Go work today in my vineyard." The son replied, "I will not," but later changed his mind and went. Jesus would have us regard him an obedient son. Similarly, there have been missionaries who after initial words of refusal bethought themselves and obeyed the divine call. Jonah was different in that he said nothing but silently ran away from an assignment. This was disobedience which God could not countenance.

In attempting to escape from the Lord, Jonah went to Joppa and boarded a freighter bound for Tarshish. This port city, it is believed, was located on the far western end of the Mediterranean Sea, probably in Southern Spain not far from Gibraltar. The sea journey, Jonah thought, would take him so far away from home and his assigned field that his escape would be complete. He did not reckon with the all-seeing eye of God. He left out of account the impossibility of hiding from the Universal Presence. The psalmist declares: "Whither shall I go from Thy Spirit, or whither shall I flee from Thy presence? If I ascend up into heaven, Thou art there. If I make my bed in hell, behold, Thou art there. If I take the wings of the morning and dwell in the uttermost parts of the sea, even there shall Thy hand lead me and Thy right hand shall hold me." This trust Jonah forgot.

We know how God foiled Jonah's attempt at flight, namely, by sending a tempest. When at the height of the storm the mariners cast the prophet into the sea, God prepared a great fish to swallow him. God took wind, water, and a creature of the deep into His miraculous employ to carry out His purpose with regard to Jonah's mission. The events contributed to a most newsworthy miracle, for instead of a man catching a fish, it was a fish catching a man. To such length God will go to implement His gracious will toward Jonah, whom He saved from drowning, and toward the people of Nineveh, whom He would lead to repentance.

The experience at sea, which for Jonah included time for prayer, meditation, and a reconsideration of his "no," had the effect of righting the wrong-way missionary. During the three days and three nights in the belly of the fish the renegade prophet had opportunity to reevaluate his relation to God. In answer to his prayer for deliverance God saved him. There was, as Jonah now realized, a definite purpose God wanted him to fulfill. He had learned, as he testified in his prayer, that his "salvation is of the Lord," also that the salvation of the Ninevites was God's steadfast intent. Consequently, when the second call

[87]

came: "Arise, go unto Nineveh, that great city, and preach unto it the preaching that I bid thee," Jonah's response was immediate. Almost as an echo of God's words comes the report of the prophet's obedience: "So Jonah arose and went unto Nineveh, according to the word of the Lord."

God has on many other occasions righted wrong-way missionaries. When Paul and Silas were moving in the wrong direction in Phrygia and the region of Galatia on the second missionary journey, they "were forbidden of the Holy Ghost to preach the Word in Asia." Again, when they attempted to enter Bithynia, "the Spirit suffered them not." God made it evident that He had another mission field in mind. In answer to the Macedonian call, which was communicated to Paul in a vision, the apostle and his colleague crossed over into Europe and found many open doors.

Sometimes God stops missionaries, not because their direction is wrong but their intent is false. For the latter reason He will not let some false prophets reach their destination. In the Book of Numbers we read the rather strange story of Balaam, who made this excellent response when Balak of the Moabites wanted him to curse the Children of Israel: "If Balak would give me his house full of silver and gold, I cannot go beyond the word of the Lord, my God, to do less or more." However, in the morning Balaam weakened and set out with Balak's men, presumably to utter the curse. On an improper mission, the wrong-way prophet found his progress barred, for "the angel of the Lord stood in the way for an adversary against him." When Balaam, on being chided by his ass, was ready to turn back, the angel sent him on his mission with the instruction to speak God's Word only. The eventual outcome was Balaam's utterance of this blessing and Messianic prophecy: "There shall come a Star out of Jacob, and a Scepter shall rise out of Israel, and shall smite the corners of Moab."

When missionaries go the wrong way, it is not always because of disobedience or fear. It may be due to improper planning, inadequate evaluation of the prospects of the mission field, or simply to the human factor of honest fallibility. Even under the best of circumstances man is limited in his knowledge, as were Paul and Silas in Asia Minor. He is very apt to make mistakes, mistakes which occur despite his best intentions. Christian missionaries are willing to take guidance from God. If shown to be wrong, they will gladly retrace their steps and go to fields which the Lord opens to them.

The story of Jonah prompts the question, Who is a missionary? Every Christian is a disciple of Jesus Christ and thus a missionary. Whatever his vocation or station, his mission in life is to accede to the Savior's commission to make disciples of other people. Not only full-time workers in foreign and domestic mission fields but all Christians, by their prayers, contributions, and witness bearing, are missionaries where they are. Christian housewives, truck drivers, business executives, college students, and others in their several callings are associates in the mission of the church. We are all in it together.

But what happens when Christians in various walks of life fail to be Christ's witnesses? What if they say, "This is the ministers' and missionaries' job"? What if they retreat from the duties and opportunities of their soul-winning vocation and refuse to speak a word for Jesus? What if, instead of going to a home where Christian testimony, exhortation, or consolation is needed, they turn around and go the other way? Is that not a repetition of the action of Jonah, the wrong-way missionary? It does not become those who may also have been remiss or disobedient to cast stones at Jonah. Let us rather profit from his experience and resolve, with God helping us, to reverse our misdirected steps and walk the paths of God's will and pleasure.

II

Jonah Became a Missionary When He Understood that God Would Rather Save than Destroy Sinners

In response to his second summons Jonah went to Nineveh, the capital city of the hostile Assyrian Empire. He found it "an exceeding great city of three days' journey." Venturing in about a third of the way, he began to publish his message, to wit, that Nineveh would fall in 40 days. What effect did his words have? An amazing thing happened, showing the power of the Word of God, much to the prophet's surprise. The people gave heed to the warning, proclaiming a fast and donning the sackcloth of penitence. The reaction was like a ground swell, like a movement beginning at the grassroots. The repentance wave spread even to the palace. The king laid aside his royal robes and garbed himself in mourning apparel. A time of prayer was announced, each citizen being besought to "cry mightily unto God" in the hope of averting the doom.

The Ninevites' change of heart was followed by a change in the Lord's announced plans. Formerly the city's wickedness came up before God; now it was a wave of the prayers of penitence. In His mercy God resolved to extend the time of grace instead of wiping out the inhabitants. This new development brought no joy to the misguided missionary from the land of Israel. Instead of rejoicing with the angels of heaven at the repentance of so many sinners, Jonah was both displeased and angry. So chagrined was he that he wished to die.

How are we to explain this strange attitude in a supposed soul winner? An important clue is found in Jonah's remonstrating reply to God. It indicated that the prophet all along was not in sympathy with the Lord's purpose to bring about the conversion of Israel's national enemy. In effect Jonah said, "Lord, now You know why I ran off to Tarshish. I realized all the time that You are a gracious God and would not go through with the threatened destruction of the city. I am not in favor of showing mercy to the enemies of my people."

It is thus made clear why Jonah was a wrong-way missionary going west instead of east. His heart was not properly constituted. His feet went the wrong way because his heart was polarized toward hatred rather than love. In this state of emotions Jonah could not be a helpful missionary despite his physical presence and his preaching in Nineveh. Only then could he be an effective instrument in God's hand when he realized that God would rather save than destroy these people. By sharing in the love of God the Ninevite missionary would love sinners, too, and then a blessed ministry could begin.

How was the prophet to be brought around to the Lord's point of view? The object lesson of the gourd was to effect this change of heart. Let us see how the incident of the gourd figures into the story. Jonah had taken up temporary residence on Nineveh's east side, where in the shadow of his booth he awaited the outcome of what he considered the pending fate of the city. The booth provided him with protection against the burning rays of the directly overhead sun. It did not shield him, however, from the slanting rays of the rising sun. How pleased was Jonah therefore when during the night a leafy gourd had quickly grown out of the ground and climbed the makeshift trellis. But the hospitable gourd was not to last long. The Lord gave it and the Lord took it away. Bitten by a worm, the gourd withered and died, leaving the brooding prophet exposed to the merciless sun and a vehement east wind. Jonah regretted deeply the passing of a plant, although he had neither planted nor cultivated it. He was grief-stricken to death over the loss of a gourd which, with its brief career from one night to the next, could not compare in value with the immortal souls of men.

What point did the Lord want to drive home with the untimely demise of the gourd? He confronted Jonah with an argument from the lesser to the greater. If the prophet was heartbroken because an ephemeral gourd died, how much more would it not grieve the heart of the heavenly Father if so many people of Nineveh, both adults and children, were to perish? The account of Jonah ends with this question: "Should not I spare Nineveh, that great city, wherein are more than sixscore thousand persons that cannot discern between their right hand and their left hand?" Nothing is reported of Jonah's reaction to the object lesson. We can be sure that the prophet got the point and showed improvement in his attitude. The very fact that he himself gives us a detailed progress report of the betterment of his misconceptions indicates this. With a heart filled with compassion for mankind Jonah could now begin to do effective work as a missionary.

There is an important lesson for us also in this phase of Jonah's story. Right-way missionaries are Christian men and women who not only go to their assigned fields of labor but also have at heart the spiritual welfare of the people, whether they are their friends or their enemies. They are dedicated workers in whom a similitude of the heart of God dwells. As the heavenly Father loves, so they love. The great theme of the Holy Scriptures is the compassion of God for sinners. In Ezekiel's prophecy we read: "Have I any pleasure at all that the wicked should die? saith the Lord God, and not that he should return from his ways and live?" Peter teaches the same in the Second Epistle: "The Lord is not willing that any should perish, but that all should come to repentance." Likewise St. Paul writes to Timothy: "God will have all men to be saved and to come unto the knowledge of the truth."

But how saved? In this passage from First Timothy the apostle continues, "For there is one God and one Mediator between God and men, the man Christ Jesus, who gave Himself a ransom for all." Jesus gave His very life on the cross for the salvation of all men. It is in Christ, the Redeemer, that God is "a gracious God and merciful, slow to anger, and of great kindness." This very truth that Jonah in his erstwhile blindness resented is the heart of the Biblical religion and the force impelling right-way missionaries to go to the ends of the earth as messengers of salvation.

Right-way, right-minded missionaries will go anywhere the Lord sends them, because they, like their Father in heaven, have no pleasure in the death of the wicked, but desire that the wicked repent, believe in the Lord Jesus Christ, and live. They will go to the bastions of unbelief, to Satan's citadels of idolatry, to the jungles of untamed savages. If God so directs them, they will go to Moscow, Peiping, Havana, and other capitals of communist countries. Political and racial prejudices at home or abroad do not hinder them from proclaiming the Word which saves men's souls. By this willingness they show themselves missionaries in whom dwell the love of God and real concern for the welfare of sinners.

[93]

Jonah on two counts consulted with his own flesh and blood and made grievous mistakes. His first mistake was the attempt to evade his divine commission by fleeing to parts unknown instead of going to his appointed mission parish. His second mistake was his displeasure at the Lord's gracious purpose to spare penitent sinners. These mistakes made him a wrong-way missionary. It was only after the Lord righted him that he could be a witness and workman in the world-encompassing kingdom of the Lord.

The story of Jonah suggests a third mistake, namely, the prophet's unwillingness to believe that a lone Hebrew prophet from a despised and hated country could accomplish anything with his preaching in "that great city." This supposition left out of account the power of the Word of God. Indeed, one man working in so populous a city, if left to his own human resources, would have met with dismal failure. But Jonah was not alone or left to his own devices. He was armed with the most potent weapon a man of God can bear, namely, the sword of the Spirit, which is the Word of God. The story of Jonah shows the wonderful results of the preaching of God's Word, results which the Holy Spirit works. We in our day are greatly encouraged to proclaim the Gospel because we, too, have occasion to see the fruits of the Word in many lands. The light of the Word is everywhere dispelling the darkness of sin, as Peter reminds us: "We have also a more sure Word of prophecy, whereunto ye do well that ye take heed, as unto a light that shineth in a dark place, until the day dawn and the Daystar arise in your hearts." May we always sow the seed of the Word faithfully in the firm confidence that God will give the increase.

MICAH

New Use for War Weapons

But in the last days it shall come to pass that the mountain of the house of the Lord shall be established in the top of the mountains, and it shall be exalted above the hills; and people shall flow unto it. And many nations shall come and say, Come and let us go up to the mountain of the Lord, and to the house of the God of Jacob; and He will teach us of His ways, and we will walk in His paths; for the Law shall go forth of Zion and the Word of the Lord from Jerusalem. And He shall judge among many people, and rebuke strong nations afar off; and they shall beat their swords into plowshares and their spears into pruning hooks; nation shall not lift up a sword against nation, neither shall they learn war anymore. But they shall sit every man under his vine and under his fig tree; and none shall make them afraid; for the mouth of the Lord of hosts hath spoken it.

Micah 4:1-4

WHEN A WAR IS OVER, there is the problem of what to do with remaining military supplies, such as armored cars, trucks, weapons, uniforms, woolen blankets, and various other equipment. Many of these things cannot be used in civilian life during peacetime. Without much salvage, they are simply disposed of at great monetary loss. On the other hand, there are also war materials that can be converted to civilian use. They can be bought in Army surplus stores. Among military vehicles that could be used in peacetime occupations was the Army jeep. It was originally developed for transportation in rugged battle areas where roads were difficult, if at all existent. When the war ended, it was found that the jeep would be a useful vehicle on farms, oil fields, and construction jobs. Even after the war the company continued to manufacture the jeep, with various improvements and conveniences, for civilian pursuits. We have here a good example of war equipment converted to peaceful use. The jeep reminds us of a similar conversion taking place in a spiritual sense, as Micah states: "They shall beat their swords into plowshares and their spears into pruning hooks." This thought we want to extend as we present New Use for War Weapons: (1) Man wages war against God; (2) Christ makes peace; (3) His subjects serve Him with new hearts.

I

Man Wages War Against God

In the preceding portion of his book Micah describes the spiritual war that Judah and its capital city, Jerusalem, waged against God. He charges that they did this with their transgressions and sins, chiefly with idolatry. There was other irreligion. Those who were supposed to be prophets and priests taught falsely and from false motives. Micah writes: "The priests thereof teach for hire, and the prophets thereof divine for money." What a sorry state! You ask a priest or prophet, "Why are you doing this work?" and he brazenly replies: "For money."

There was among the people in general an unashamed covetousness contrary to the Ninth Commandment. "They covet fields and take them by violence; and houses, and take them away," the prophet declares. In the same vein, Micah exposes

[96]

this merciless exploitation, showing the ongoing war: "Even of late my people is risen up as an enemy; ye pull off the robe with the garment from them that pass by securely as men averse from war."

How is it with chieftains and princes? They also are materially-minded. The prophet tells them: You "hate the good and love the evil; who pluck off their skin from off them, and their flesh from off their bones." What little regard the rulers have for their subjects! In a continuous civilian war they deprive the people of the means of life and of life itself.

When man does not love God, he sins against the commandments on the First Table. When he does not love his neighbor, he sins against the commandments on the Second Table. In either case he opposes the will of God and wages spiritual war. This, as the prophet shows, was a sin not only peculiar to the land of Judah. Also in heathen lands there is enmity against God and opposition to the Moral Law written in man's heart. God is therefore also the Judge of all mankind, as Micah states in the text: "He shall judge among many people and rebuke strong nations afar off."

How did this warfare against God begin? It began, of all places, in heaven, where the devil and his angels rebelled against God. John reminds of this in the Book of Revelation, saying: "There was war in heaven: Michael and his angels fought against the dragon; and the dragon fought and his angels, and prevailed not; neither was their place found anymore in heaven." Indeed, heaven purged itself of this rebellion against God.

The devil, cast out of heaven, brought the warfare of sin to this world. He who sinned from the beginning and abode not in the truth succeeded in involving Adam and Eve in a master lie. Under the spell of temptation, man in the Garden of Eden rejected the rule of God and set up his own kingdom. Ever since that time sin-fallen man's reaction to God's holy will has been the same. Where God says, "Do it," man says, "I won't." To God's "Don't do it" he replies with "I will."

Every disobedience represents man's refusal to be on God's side. Instead of being spiritually minded man is carnally minded, and that state of mind is enmity against God. Instead of loving the light he loves darkness, and that is a declaration of war against God, who is the Light. Instead of doing what is good, man, like Judah's princes, loves the evil, and that is a sure sign of his defection to the side of the devil.

In our times, too, we see how man opposes himself to God and God's Word. Not only the communist man does this; not only the criminal man. The so-called free man living in a free society manifests his insurrection by abusing freedom. When God speaks to him, he replies, "I have freedom to do as I please." When a commandment or a doctrine does not please such a libertine, he simply rejects it or conveniently forgets about it. Whether he realizes it or not, he is taking up weapons against God.

Are we Christians entirely free of the warfare that Satan and the world wage against God as the highest Authority? Regrettably, we are not, for the sinful flesh still lurking in our members is hostile to God. Wherever there is sin, there is war against God and His people. James probes deeply but discerningly into the human heart when he propounds these questions to his Christian readers: "From whence come wars and fightings among you? Come they not hence, even of your lusts that war in your members?" He

[98]

proceeds to show that lust-born wars and fightings are sins not only against the neighbor but against God as well. Therefore God will resist those who engage in war against their brethren.

II

Christ Makes Peace

Judah and Jerusalem had carried on spiritual warfare against God, but for the pious remnant in the land and for converted heathen assembling in Zion peace is proclaimed. "They shall sit every man under his vine and under his fig tree; and none shall make them afraid; for the mouth of the Lord of hosts hath spoken it," Micah prophesied. Isaiah, a contemporary of Micah, had also spoken of spiritual peace in the days of the Messiah in these words: "Speak ye comfortably to Jerusalem and cry unto her that her warfare is accomplished, that her iniquity is pardoned; for she hath received of the Lord's hand double for all her sins." These are references to the Kingdom of Grace and rule of peace under the Messiah.

There are clear prophecies of the coming Messiah in Micah's testimony. At the end of chapter two the prophet declared: "The Breaker is come up before them; they have broken up and have passed through the gate and are gone out by it; and their King shall pass before them, and the Lord on the head of them." The "breaker," translated by Luther as the "Durchbrecher," is the One who effects the "breakthrough," ends the impasse of sin's dominion, and opens the gate to peace. In the fifth chapter the identification of the Breaker and Ruler is even more clearly made, namely, in the familiar passage: "But thou, Bethlehem Ephratah, though thou be little among the thousands of Judah, yet out of thee shall He come forth unto

Me that is to be Ruler in Israel; whose goings forth have been from of old, from everlasting." That cannot be a prophecy of a temporal prince, for the Bethlehem-born ruler is "from everlasting." Without question the Scripture, as also the scribe-consultants of King Herod knew, here testifies of Jesus Christ, the Messiah, born in Bethlehem.

Under the rule of the Prince of Peace there is to come to pass the reversal of a dominant situation. From spiritual warfare men shall turn to peace. Since history records over 800 wars, many of them fought since Micah wrote these words, the reference cannot be to temporal peace. What is here visualized is the peace of the New Testament era as mediated by Jesus Christ. As Peacemaker and Mediator between God and men our blessed Lord became incarnate that He might fulfill the Law in the sinners' stead, offering to God His obedience for men's disobedience. What is more, as Substitute for us and as Captain of our salvation He entered into warfare against sin, death, and the devil. In the great battle that reached its climax on Calvary's cross He laid down His life. He did this of His own free will and in perfect love for all mankind. The life our Savior so freely surrendered He was, of course, able to assume again on the third day after His entombment. On Easter morning He rose again from the dead, thus proclaiming not only His victory but also the peace He had won. The resurrection seals all benefits accruing to us from the Atonement, specifically that "the chastisement of our peace was upon Him and that with His stripes we are healed." Christ was, as also St. Paul teaches, "delivered for our offenses and was raised again for our justification." It was therefore a most meaningful greeting the risen Lord addressed to His disciples when He said, "Peace be unto you."

MICAH

The peace with God issues in peace among men. Reconciled with God, we cannot but be reconciled one with another. The old enmity between Jews and Gentiles over the Law is taken away, for it is no longer in the Law but in Him who fulfilled the Law that their common faith rests. Thus in a very appropriate application of the Gospel to a human situation was St. Paul able to heal an ugly wound in the early church, namely, the threatening breach between Christians of Jewish and Gentile extraction. He tells both parties: "For He is our Peace, who hath made both one and hath broken down the middle wall of partition between us, having abolished in His flesh the enmity, even the law of commandments contained in ordinances." Would that also in these times of racial tensions full use were made of the Gospel to bring people together! The law is divisive, but in Christ there is no East and West, no North and South.

The peace that Christ has gained for all people and all nations He wants us to proclaim in all lands. Our Lord would have us go and teach all nations. In obedience to His will the messengers of peace have gone to all the world to make known His "saving health among nations." What a blessing they have been because they published the Gospel of peace! Isaiah exclaims: "How beautiful upon the mountains are the feet of him that bringeth good tidings, that publisheth peace; that bringeth good tidings of good, that publisheth salvation; that saith unto Zion, Thy God reigneth!"

The Zion here visualized has been augmented by the influx of many people. Micah foresaw this, saying: "But in the last days it shall come to pass that the mountain of the house of the Lord shall be established in the top of the mountains, and it shall be exalted above the hills; and people shall flow unto it."

God has truly enlarged and elevated His spiritual Zion, the New Testament church. It is like a city on a high hill that cannot be hid. The hills of man-made religions still stand, being in our day surpassed by communism and other economic-political systems offered as substitutes for religion, but the Christian church overshadows them all. From every nation come representatives who would serve the true God, saying to each other as they make the journey of faith, "Come and let us go up to the mountain of the Lord, and to the house of the God of Jacob; and He will teach us of His ways, and we will walk in His paths."

III

His Subjects Serve Him with New Hearts

When these nations come to worship Christ, they do not bring weapons of war but the instruments of peaceful service. What have they done with their war equipment? Micah prophesies that "they shall beat their swords into plowshares and their spears into pruning hooks." These words, to be taken in a spiritual sense, bespeak the new use of war weapons. What is the prophet saying in these symbolic terms? The same that St. Paul said in Romans: "Neither yield ye your members as instruments [alternate translation: arms, or weapons] of unrighteousness unto sin; but yield yourselves unto God, as those that are alive from the dead, and your members as instruments of righteousness unto God."

The greatest of all conversions of spiritual weapons is, of course, the transformation of the heart, as the apostle states: "Yield *yourselves* unto God." Then follows that we yield to the service of Christ also the members of our bodies. The best example of total conversion to Christ is Paul himself. Before becoming a Christian, Saul the Pharisee threw everything he had into the battle against Christ: His heart, mind, reason, hands, feet, and all bodily members. Every personal power, every possible resource he could get his hands on he used as sword and spear to fight Christianity. But after Paul became a Christian and the sword of the Spirit was pressed into his hand, he devoted heart, mind, and body to the upbuilding of Christ's kingdom. It was like a man beating his sword into a plowshare and his spear into a pruning hook.

We, too, as the servants of the Prince of Peace, serve Him with our reconverted weapons. This spiritual armory includes the heart, the seat of what we really are and what we think, desire, speak, and do. Our heart, where once we were estranged from Christ, we now give Him in fervent love. Along with the heart the Holy Spirit has also converted our minds, and with these wonderful instruments we now serve Christ. There are all the members of the body, once the instruments of sin and weapons with which to fight God. Now we serve with them: with hands, to do His work; with feet, to walk His paths and to carry His message to all nations; with eyes, to behold His wonders; with ears, to hear His Word; with mouths, to praise Him and to speak for Him. Former servants of sin though we may have been, we yield our members servants to righteousness unto holiness. This is the new use of former war weapons.

Men by nature are enemies of God and spiritual warmongers, because they are blind, dead in sin, and carnally minded. For such, while they were yet enemies, Christ died, reconciling them to God. Through the Gospel the Holy Spirit changes hostile hearts, instills faith, and kindles love, so that as Christ's peace soldiers they serve Him now with all their hearts, souls, minds, and strength. This is the peace service to which also Peter calls us when he writes: "Forasmuch then as Christ hath suffered for us in the flesh, arm yourselves likewise with the same mind; for he that hath suffered in the flesh hath ceased from sin, that he no longer should live the rest of his time in the flesh to the lusts of men, but to the will of God."

NAHUM

A Message from the Mountains

*Behold upon the mountains the feet of him that bring-
eth good tidings, that publisheth peace! O Judah, keep
thy solemn feasts, perform thy vows; for the wicked shall
no more pass through thee; he is utterly cut off.*

Nahum 1:15

MOUNTAINS HAVE MESSAGES for man. For the young,
"Springtime in the Rockies" brings tidings of romance.
John Muir encourages both young and old, "Climb
the mountains and get their good tidings. Nature's
peace will flow into you as sunshine flows into the
trees." Mountains speak to Christians not only of the
majesty of the Creator but also of God's love in Christ.
The Sangre de Cristo ("Blood of Christ") range in
Colorado, especially the Mount of the Holy Cross,
whose snow-filled crevasses form the outline of a white
cross, remind of redemption.

Rudyard Kipling thought of mountains as having
secret messages which explorers must seek out. He
writes,

> Something hidden — go and find it;
> Go and look behind the Ranges.
> Something lost behind the Ranges;
> Lost and waiting for you. Go.

Mountains played prominent roles in the lives of
people spoken of in the Bible. As pilgrims neared

[105]

Jerusalem at the time of the high festivals, they thrilled to the sight of the holy mounts. As they looked up, they were reminded that all help comes from God. Thus they sang: "I will lift up mine eyes unto the hills, from whence cometh my help. My help cometh from the Lord, which made heaven and earth." There was a time when God's people in Jerusalem again looked to the mountains for a message of deliverance from Assyrian oppressors. It is also from on high that the Good News of man's redemption from spiritual enemies comes. Nahum speaks of this as he bids us consider A Message from the Mountains: (1) The message as an announcement of Divine Grace; (2) the desired effect of the message.

I

The Message as an Announcement of Divine Grace

The prophecy of Nahum recounts the struggle of two cities, Nineveh and Jerusalem. Nineveh, the capital of the Assyrian Empire under King Sennacherib, is described as a "bloody city." Her soldiers, called emptiers, had emptied the Northern Kingdom, carrying into captivity the "excellency of Israel." They threatened to do the same to the Southern Kingdom and its capital, Jerusalem. However, Nahum predicted doom for Nineveh. While it yet flourished in all its cruel might, he said, "Nineveh is laid waste." This prophecy was fulfilled to the letter. Nineveh was long ago wiped off the face of the earth. The other city, which was the scene of Nahum's activity, is still in existence. It is Jerusalem, to whom the prophet, according to the Hebrew meaning of his name, was a comforter. Nahum's name, "rich in comfort is God," proclaims the Old Testament Gospel in a nutshell.

[106]

What comfort does Nahum have for the besieged people of God? The prophet promises that news of the defeat of the enemy will come. The tidings of peace will be brought by messengers crossing the mountains. The meaning of the message is not only political or secular. Contained in it are the tidings of spiritual deliverance, as is clearly established by Saint Paul's use of this passage. In Romans 10 the apostle speaks of the need of commissioning messengers to preach the Word of God, supporting the point from the words of our text, which are also found in Isaiah 52:7: "How beautiful are the feet of them that preach the Gospel of peace, and bring glad tidings of good things!"

The essence of the gladsome message is the Gospel. It is the announcement of divine grace and forgiveness. What the messengers publish is peace, peace with God, reconciliation. It presupposes a peacemaker or mediator, for whose sake God now thinks "thoughts of peace and not of evil" toward mankind. This peacemaker is identified by Isaiah as the Messiah, Jehovah's Servant, whom he calls the Prince of Peace. Isaiah also tells us how the Messiah became the Peacemaker, namely, through His suffering and death in our behalf. His teaching is very plain: "The chastisement of our peace was upon Him, and with His stripes we are healed."

On the basis of what the prophets taught in the Scriptures, the apostles likewise preached peace, namely, the peace that Jesus Christ procured. The spokesmen, from the vantage point of fulfillment, reasoned from the Scriptures that Jesus of Nazareth is the Redeemer of whom the prophets testified. All that God would do for the salvation of mankind He did through the incarnation, death, and resurrection of Jesus Christ. Clear and unanimous is their testimony. Peter preached: "Neither is there salvation in any other, for there is none other name under heaven given among men, whereby we must be saved." As from a mountaintop Paul proclaims: "God hath delivered us from the power of darkness and hath translated us into the kingdom of His dear Son, in whom we have redemption through His blood, even the forgiveness of sins."

Because there was this message, there could be a mission, namely, the proclamation of the grace of God in Jesus Christ. It was for preaching this truth that Christ sent forth His disciples to Jerusalem, Judea, Samaria, and the uttermost part of the earth. Crossing lands and seas, indeed "field and fountain, moor and mountain," they published this peace.

What a joyful announcement these witnesses of Christ in both the Old and the New Testament could proclaim! As Nahum of old and his near contemporary, Isaiah, who is called the "evangelist of the Old Testament," they were comforters and bearers of good tidings. From the sloughs of sin, from the valleys of the shadow of death, people in all ages could look up to the mountains and behold the coming of messengers. From afar they could tell that the couriers bring good news, for they came posthaste. The joy of heart moves the feet to move more quickly. What a welcome sight to see the messengers of divine love come over the elevated ridges with tidings of deliverance! Little wonder that mankind exults: "How beautiful are the feet of them that preach the Gospel of peace!" Feet are not the most comely members of the body. However, when they are shod with the preparation of the Gospel of peace, they are lovely indeed.

[108]

We are living in times when man's messengers bring increasingly worse news of human degradation and grave world conditions resulting from it. They are like the couriers who told Job, one after another: The Sabeans took away the oxen and asses and slew the servants; fire from heaven consumed the sheep and the shepherds; the Chaldeans fell on camels and cameleers; and a great wind from the wilderness wiped out the entire family. The bad news today is that communism is making advances on all fronts, nationalism is running rampant in newborn countries, ever and ever more fearsome weapons are being perfected, morals are sagging, many are ready to capitulate to the enemy, and many more discouraging reports. Against the dark background of evil tidings God still proclaims the message of His mercy in Christ. How welcome this Good News is!

But is it welcome? Does mankind everywhere hail with joy the coming of Christian missionaries? It does not. This is true: Because of spiritual blindness and the seed of hatred sown by the enemies of Christianity, Christ's messengers in many lands are told, "Go home." This is, of course, not a new development. It was so in the days of the prophets and the apostles. Men steeped in sin and held captive by Satan have always resented the coming of spokesmen preaching spiritual liberation.

We must expect that today natives will close doors to missionaries, that our own counrtymen, preoccupied with earthly concerns, will show indifference rather than joy at the communication of Christ's Gospel. There will be poor reception until the hearts of sin-hardened mankind are prepared for the Gospel by the intervention of the Holy Spirit. And God is active in the affairs of the world. When sorrows are heaped on sorrows, disappointments multiply, and man's last hope of self-sufficiency is gone, a great moment for the kingdom of God has come. When 20th-century man has come to realize fully his misery in sin, as certainly the people of Jerusalem had because of corruption within and military attacks from without, the ground has been prepared for the seed of the Gospel. It is then that man, quickened in hope by the Holy Spirit, hails the good tidings of grace. This is then also the time for the church to take to the mountains with its message of salvation, as Isaiah urges: "O Zion, that bringeth good tidings, get thee up into the high mountain; O Jerusalem, that bringest good tidings, lift up thy voice with strength; lift it up, be not afraid; say unto the cities of Judah, Behold your God!"

II

The Desired Effect of the Message

It lies in the very nature of the message of grace that it will bring about changes in the hearts and lives of those who accept it. What are the desired effects? Nahum encouraged Judah, as the Old Testament church: "Keep thy solemn feasts." Because of war conditions the spiritual activities of God's people in Jerusalem were greatly circumscribed, if not discontinued altogether. Disturbances in the world have their effect on the church. This happens also today when a calamity strikes a community. Who can celebrate Christmas, for example, in a normal way when a city is under bombardment? How can there be Easter festivities when a fire runs wild or homes and churches are flooded? During such times church services and special holy-day events are suspended. However, with the passing of the crisis it is time to

resume normal church activities. That is what Nahum
wants Judah to do, namely: Keep again the solemn
festivals! Reinstitute worship! Let the Passover, the
Feast of Weeks, the Feast of Tabernacles, the Day of
Atonement, and other holy occasions be restored!
Above all, call a solemn assembly for thanksgiving,
now that the siege has lifted!

In the Epistle generally read on Easter Sunday
St. Paul urges us to "keep the feast." In laying the
doctrinal basis for this act of joyful worship he tells
us: "Christ, our Passover, is sacrificed for us." Not only
was Christ offered on the cross as the Passover Lamb,
but He also rose again from the dead to set the seal
of sufficiency on His sacrifice. His death and resurrection not only establish articles of faith but also
have significance for Christian life. The desired effect
of all that Christ did for our salvation is that we purge
out the old leaven of sin and live by the unleavened
bread of sincerity and truth.

Apart from Easter, we as the New Testament
church keep other solemn feasts in celebration of
the great acts of God for our salvation. It is meet and
right to do so, with the understanding, of course, that
we be more than Christmas and Easter Christians.
How pleasing it is to God when we continue to faithfully sanctify the Lord's day and assemble for other
worshipful occasions! Worship is service to God. It is
thanksgiving and thanksliving for all spiritual blessings God multiplies to us in Christ and communicates
through the Word and the sacraments. If for some
good reason or another there is an interruption of our
worship life, we by all means want to restore the
solemn feasts. These interruptions, very likely, are
not due to the failure of the church to observe divine
feast days but to the failure of individual members

to participate in them. Thus, with regard to attendance at Sunday services and other worship situations, attendance at Holy Communion, to say nothing of the high festivals of the church year or special services in Advent and Lent, it is every Christian's personal resolve, "I shall keep the solemn feasts." As a people to whom God has announced full redemption in Christ we can do no less.

The message from the mountains was to have another effect, namely, readiness to "perform thy vows," as Nahum exhorts Judah. Perhaps some in Jerusalem had vowed to do some special thing to the glory of God if He preserved them from the peril of death or bodily harm. The good news now published gave the assurance that God had delivered them. The time is come now to perform these vows, to do what they had promised to do. Apart from special vows there was always the standing vow of the covenant whereby God promised to be Israel's God and Israel promised to be God's people. Let this vow also be kept, now that peace has returned. Nahum reechoes here the words of the psalmist: "Praise waiteth for Thee, O God, in Zion, and unto Thee shall the vow be performed."

We Christians, too, make vows. There is the baptismal vow, the confirmation vow, the marriage vow. In these vows we solemnly promise, with God as our witness, to remain faithful to Him and to one another until death. It is a sad fact that some church members take these vows lightly. Despite their vows, willingly and freely given, they act contrary to them or reject them altogether. The result is many apostasies from the faith, many broken marriages.

A Christian who has received the tidings of forgiveness in Christ and has become God's child cannot but take to heart Nahum's exhortation to perform his vow. The same is true of pledges made to God's glory and furtherance of His kingdom. Some pledges of a personal nature have value for the individual but cannot be enforced on all, such as the "temperance pledge," which usually means the "total abstinence pledge." Nevertheless, if a person has taken such a pledge, let him perform it, particularly if he has reason to think that he cannot use strong drink in moderation. Not all pledges are commendable. A pledge that a Christian will refrain from making is one he may not in good conscience be able to keep, such as the solemn promise given to a dying marriage partner never to marry again. The question as to whether to do or not to do had at that moment better be left to God.

A pledge which a church member will by all means try to keep is the written promise to contribute financially in a self-stipulated amount and as God has blessed him. Why should it be taken seriously? The congregation locally and the church at large have commitments to fulfill. They cannot fulfill them unless individual members make good on their promises. Pledging one's gifts to the Lord's work implies forethought and planning, followed by performance. This is certainly the meaning of Paul's words: "Upon the first day of the week let every one of you lay by him in store, as God hath prospered him." It is, of course, another matter when something unforeseen arises, making it impossible for a church member to contribute the contemplated amount. In such emergencies a contribution pledge made in good faith is not to be regarded as equivalent to an oath or a promissory note. Apart from emergencies, a good rule to follow is: "Perform thy pledge."

Keeping the solemn feasts and performing vows are phases of Christian sanctification and service. There are many other ministrations to which Christians are motivated by the Good News of total salvation coming from Mount Calvary. An important one is: As we have received the Gospel, so let us be the Lord's feet and mouth to communicate it to others. Another is, As Christ has so immeasurably enriched and served me, so will I serve the least of His brethren and communicate to them. Still another is, As we have received peace with God, so let us be at peace with one another. All these instances of Christian living and serving are responses to the love of God declared and delivered to us in the Gospel. They are the desired effects of God's announcement of grace.

God's message from the mountains — Mount Calvary, the Mount of Olives, the Mount of the Ascension — is the proclamation of divine favor and forgiveness. Its desired effect is wholehearted Christian service. The great incentive is always God's love in Christ. Nahum in the text adds a subsidiary incentive: "For the wicked shall no more pass through thee; he is utterly cut off." In a spiritual sense, it is a blessed fact that Christ has overcome all our enemies, as God said through Hosea: "I will ransom them from the power of the grave; I will redeem them from death. O death, I will be thy plagues; O grave, I will be thy destruction." These words under the inspired hand of St. Paul receive their proper, positive spiritual significance, namely, the Christian's triumph in and for Christ: "Death is swallowed up in victory. O death, where is thy sting? O grave, where is thy victory? The sting of death is sin; and the strength of sin is the Law. But thanks be to God, which giveth us the victory through our Lord Jesus Christ."

HABAKKUK

The Believer's Survival Kit

Behold, his soul which is lifted up is not upright in him; but the just shall live by his faith. Yea also, because he transgresseth by wine, he is a proud man, neither keepeth at home, who enlargeth his desire as hell, and is as death, and cannot be satisfied, but gathereth unto him all nations, and heapeth unto him all people.

Habakkuk 2:4, 5

MEN MAROONED for many days at sea or in the wilderness have been able to sustain themselves because they were equipped with survival kits. Such emergency packets may contain a limited stock of concentrated food, first-aid materials, means of protection against the elements, communication devices, and the like. These supplies can spell the difference between life and death.

Survival is one of the key words in the vocabulary of civilian-defense authorities. It bespeaks the presence of danger. Turbulence in the world has always occasioned the necessity of taking measures for self-preservation. Since the whole man is involved, the perils touch both his body and soul. Jeremiah states: "We got our bread with the peril of our lives because of the sword of the wilderness." Of spiritual dangers the psalmist says: "Save me, O God; for the waters are come in unto my soul."

[115]

Habakkuk lived in times of great international upheavals, what with the Chaldeans soon to pounce on the Holy Land "as the eagle that hasteth to eat." Since the invaders were given also to idolatry, the religious confusion already in the land would be worse confounded. What counsel has the prophet for spiritual survival amid so "many a conflict, many a doubt, fightings and fears, within, without"? His declaration of hope and confidence is simply: "The just shall live by his faith." For sustaining and saving faith there is no substitute. Faith is the Christian's "must" in times normal and abnormal. This is the lesson before us: The Believer's Survival Kit: (1) The works of pride do not prevail; (2) faith in Christ's righteousness alone saves.

I

The Works of Pride Do Not Prevail

The just person stands in sharp contrast to the proud person. The latter has a soul or spirit "which is lifted up." He is the kind of individual who without warrant or basis in fact exalts himself, glosses over his imperfections, and denies his sin. The truth is that "there is not a just man upon the earth that doeth good and sinneth not." John's judgment is: "If we say that we have no sin, we deceive ourselves, and the truth is not in us." Thus it must be added that the proud man's soul "is not upright in him." Pride feasts on false values and is to be equated with deception and lack of uprightness. Jeremiah prophesies to the Ammonite nation that "the pride of thine heart hath deceived thee." The pride of life, John bids us remember, "is not of the Father, but is of the world," the world ever crooked and perverse.

Man's ego is sometimes in need of means of sup-

[116]

port. Among the means frequently utilized to maintain pride is strong drink. Habakkuk makes mention of this, proceeding to say: "Yea, also, because he transgresseth by wine, he is a proud man." The composite Chaldean, as a type of sinful man in general, demonstrates his pride in many other acts of arrogance and aggression against his neighbor. It is more than a coincidence for Isaiah to associate pride and drink in this couplet of woes: "Woe unto them that are wise in their own eyes. . . . Woe unto them that are mighty to drink wine." What the result is when modern motorists stimulate their aggressive instinct with liquor is known to all who unfortunately must encounter them on streets and highways.

Man's pride, when it moves in a religious direction, expresses itself in reliance on good works for attaining salvation. Even if he were not to drink out of a bottle, the person of pharisaic propensities is under the influence of the heady wine of deceitful pride. The effect is that he believes: "I am strong and resourceful; I can save myself." Such a boaster is unwilling to bow before God, admit his helplessness, and beg for God's mercy, as did the publican in the temple. He is rather like the Pharisee, who enumerated his good works and obediences beyond the call of duty, regarding them as more than sufficient to gain God's favor. St. Paul would tell him: "Thou that makest thy boast of the Law, through breaking the Law dishonorest thou God?"

The fact is, the delusion of perfectionism notwithstanding, that the boaster of good works falls far short of keeping God's Law. Thus he not only dishonors God but also deprives himself of real assurance. Verbal boasts can be made, but do they truly convince man in his innermost soul? How can they? The Law of God bears witness, and conscience supports this

[117]

testimony, that the individual has failed many times. God's Law commands, "Do this, do it perfectly, and thou shalt live." Conscience inquires, "Have you done this?" In the inner sanctum of his heart man must acknowledge that he is far from perfect. Self-earned eternal life is entirely out of the question. By his own works or merits no one can be just in the sight of God. And because he is not just, he cannot live before God in time and in eternity.

What is the self-righteous sinner's chance of survival at the bar of divine judgment if he is equipped with good works only? Samuel Howard in the hymn "And Wilt Thou Pardon, Lord" laments his sins "of such crimson dye" and goes on to say: "So deep are they engraved, So terrible their fear: The righteous scarcely shall be saved, And where shall I appear?" Samuel Howard relied on the "blest Physician" to clean his guilty soul, and truly his soul was cleansed. Those who rely on their works and spurn the cleansing blood of the blest Physician have no hope of salvation. You would have to say their chances of survival are nil.

II

Faith in Christ's Righteousness Alone Saves

Opposite the proud man Habakkuk places the believing man, as in His parable Jesus contrasted the boastful Pharisee with the penitent publican. The prophet's contrast between the two figures is strongly indicated in the word *but* — "but the just shall live by his faith."

This is a most significant statement, repeated several times in the New Testament. St. Paul quoted it in the opening chapter of Romans to intone his exposition of the sinner's righteousness before God by faith. He writes in this connection that in the Gospel

[118]

of Christ, of which he is not ashamed, "is the right-eousness of God revealed from faith to faith" (revealed in consequence of faith and intended for faith), hold-ing that the total-faith principle was taught by Habak-kuk. Citing this Scripture, Paul adds: "As it is written, The just shall live by faith."

Further, in the third chapter of Galatians Paul discusses the impossibility of man's being justified by the Law. This impossibility, he reasons, is evident from the Law, for it declares: "Cursed is everyone that continueth not in all the things which are written in the Book of the Law to do them." It is evident, too, from the Gospel. At this point the apostle quotes the Habakkuk passage to teach justification by faith.

Finally, the Habakkuk text occurs in the tenth chapter of the Epistle to the Hebrews. The discus-sion there centers in steadfast faith amid afflictions. The writer urges his readers: "Cast not away therefore your confidence." The reason for clinging to faith is evident: it brings salvation. To prove this, the Hebrews author quotes the "Now the just shall live by faith" passage from Habakkuk.

Little wonder that this verse was so dear to Mar-tin Luther. It helped the Reformer to come to the right understanding of the doctrine of justification by faith alone. Luther's problem at first was that he could not harmonize the justice of God, which demands moral perfection, with the mercy of God, which for-gives sins. He found the key in Paul's Epistle to the Romans, where the righteousness of God is presented as the righteousness of God in Christ. Because this righteousness of Christ is imputed to the sinner through a God-given faith, that person is granted life and acceptance with God. Luther writes, "Night and day I pondered until I saw the connection between the justice of God and the statement that 'the just shall live by his faith.' Then I grasped that the justice of God is that righteousness by which through grace and sheer mercy God justifies us through faith."

Martin Luther taught the apostles' doctrine, and the apostles, in turn, built on the foundation of the Old Testament prophets. Since the Habakkuk text is a foundation stone for the doctrine of justification, it is an important utterance. Let us look at the words more closely. "But the *just*. . . ." Who can be called just? As far as uprightness of character is concerned, the Bible calls Abel, Noah, Joseph of Nazareth, and Simeon of Jerusalem just and righteous men. To the best of their ability they lived according to the Ten Commandments. What is more, Jesus speaks of the righteousness of the Pharisees. He does not question the reality of that righteousness as judged by the moral standards of Pharisaism. What He does say is that the righteousness of those who want to enter heaven must exceed that of the Pharisees.

The Book of Acts, moreover, calls Cornelius, the Roman centurion, prior to his conversion a "just man." Likewise do the Lutheran Confessions speak of civil righteousness. A person who keeps the laws of the state, avoids dishonesty, sets a good example in the community, and the like, has civil righteousness. You may call him a just man.

Is this what Habakkuk means by the *just?* Definitely not. If he did, he would declare such a man as living by his works. This he does not say, this he cannot say. By the works of the Law, God's or man's, no man can be justified. Only that man is just in the sight of God and acceptable for heaven who is garbed in the dress of Christ's righteousness. So the prophets and apostles taught of the righteousness which pre-

[120]

vails before God, "even the righteousness of God which is by faith of Jesus Christ unto all and upon all them that believe."

This is, then, to say: That man is just whose sins are forgiven for Christ's sake. Again, that is a just man who by faith accepts the righteousness of Christ as his. So it was said of Abraham, the father of the believers. Abraham had faith, and it was counted to him for righteousness. Faith is the hand that appropriates the merits of Christ — faith, which is not man's own achievement but the gift of the Holy Spirit. Faith is confidence, or reliance on Christ. The person who believes and confesses: "Jesus Christ is *my* Lord and Savior, who has redeemed me with His blood," has saving faith. He believes on the Lord Jesus Christ, and the promise applies: "Thou shalt be saved."

"Yes indeed!" said the Romanists in Reformation times, and they still say it, "we can go along with that, for a person is saved by faith." When pressed further, they show unwillingness to accept the teaching of justification by faith *alone*. They come with a "faith plus" formula: Man lives by faith *and* good works. The point clearly settled in the Reformation is that man's salvation is exclusively by faith. Good works are truly to be done, as also James teaches in his epistle, for good works outwardly express the inner life of faith. Good works, however, do not save. Salvation is by faith alone.

We have discussed who the *just* is and what *faith* means. What say the words of the text further? "The just shall *live*. . . ." The reference is not primarily to physical life or survival, although the welfare of the body is never excluded from the life God has promised to the total person. The emphasis is here on the life before God, on spiritual life in this world and on

eternal life, which believers even now possess and
shall enjoy fully in heaven. By his faith the just shall
live in the fullest sense of the word. Of the fullness
of this life Jesus said: "I am come that they might
have life, and that they might have it more abundantly." While unbelievers are dead in trespasses and
sins, Christ's disciples live under Him in His kingdom and serve Him.

May it also be said of us: They are just and truly
live by faith. This was said of the first Christians and
of the first children of the Reformation. But is faith
not often weak? Can also the struggling faith afford
survival in life's great crisis? Yes, faith is often weak,
and therefore we seek to nourish it through the means
of grace: the Word and the sacraments. The weakness
of faith should prompt us to make diligent use of the
means God has ordained for the greater vitality of
Christian faith and Christian life. When measures are
taken to strengthen faith, we need not fret about weak
faith, for it rests on Christ and is thus the saving faith.
Our prayer is: "Lord, increase our faith, that we may
live by it in this evil world and in heaven to come."

What shall we include in the whole armor of God?
What in the spiritual survival kit? Paul tells us:
"Above all, take the shield of faith."

ZEPHANIAH

Light from God's Candles

*And it shall come to pass at that time that I will
search Jerusalem with candles.*

Zephaniah 1:12

WHEN WE STEP out into the night, we see two kinds
of lights: streetlamps and stars. Man made the former, but God the latter. Streetlamps serve a good
purpose. They illuminate sidewalks and thorough-
fares so that we can see where we are going. They
dispel the cover of darkness behind which thieves and
robbers like to hide. At that, streetlamps can never
take the place of stars for the guidance of man. By
the stars you can sail across the ocean and fly an air-
plane. These heavenly bodies are still in view when
streetlamps have long disappeared. Stars signify the
might and wisdom of God, which always supersede
man's ingenuity.

For his life man must have a light which even
the stars cannot give him. That he may walk uprightly
in this world and find the way to eternal life, God
gives him a light brighter than sun, moon, and stars.
This light is His Word, as the psalmist has said: "Thy
Word is a lamp unto my feet and a light unto my
path." Keeping in mind the nature of this light, we

come to consider its effects on us. Zephaniah, in the text above, directs our attention to Light from God's Candles: (1) God's Word as a searchlight; (2) God's Word as a guiding light.

I

God's Word as a Searchlight

When we look for something in a dark room, we turn on the light. Jesus speaks in a parable of a house-wife who lighted a candle and then searched for her lost coin. Lights are for searching. Sometimes police-men cruise through the streets at night, turning their spotlights this way and that. It is evident that they are looking for someone, perhaps a lost child or a criminal hiding out.

In the text Zephaniah describes graphically how God looks for sinners with His searchlight. He writes: "At that time I will search Jerusalem with candles." During the reign of King Josiah there were many sin-ners in Jerusalem — people who in chap 1, v. 3, are described as "wicked." In a sense they were religious, but they did not worship the true God. They served Baal and Malcham, the gods of paganism. They climbed on the rooftops to worship the host of heaven, the stars. These people in Jerusalem were not heathen; they were Israelites lapsing into pagan ideas. Forsaking God, they turned to gods. So it is today. When modern man forsakes Christianity, he usually turns to other religions or to substitutes for religion. It has been said that "nature abhors a vacuum." Human nature likewise cannot endure a spiritual vacuum. When the true God is banished from the heart, some other god will be invited in.

Where pagan religions rule the day, people will conduct themselves according to the standards of

[124]

these false creeds. Because people in Jerusalem had a false faith, they had a false life. The latter is described in such terms as immorality, excessive eating, drunkenness, robbery, and deceit. Such ungodly life in Jerusalem and Judah God could not countenance. He warns of the day of visitation and judgment. This day has already been set, according to the prophet, who says: "The great day of the Lord is near, it is near, and hasteth greatly." What kind of day will it be? "A day of wrath, a day of trouble and distress, a day of wasteness and desolation, a day of darkness and gloominess, a day of clouds and thick darkness, a day of the trumpet and alarm against the fenced cities and against the high towers" (1:15, 16). It was on this text, incidentally, that Thomas de Celano of the 13th century based his Latin hymn *Dies irae, dies illa*, number 607 in *The Lutheran Hymnal*.

We see therefore that the Lord is a righteous and zealous God, who will not sit idly by or shut His eyes to the iniquity of the people. He declares: "I will search Jerusalem with candles." Who will be able to hide himself from God, who knows all and sees all, also what lies in darkness? Does He not also see the hidden thoughts of men's hearts and read them like an open book? The light of His candles and the radiance of His Word fall on every thought, word, and work.

Fellowmen cannot always see and know what others do, especially not if it is done in secret. Because human sight and knowledge do not reach that far, many evildoers feel secure amid the protection of darkness, as Jesus said: "For everyone that doeth evil hateth the light, neither cometh to the light, lest his deeds should be reproved." Such a person forgets that nothing can be kept from God. He knows the

[125]

sinner's hiding place, for He searches all Jerusalem, all the world, with candles.

To Christians does the Lord now come with His searchlight. The artist in a well-known picture shows the exalted Christ standing before the door and knocking with a lantern in His hand. Christ is the Light of the world. There is comfort in this fact, but there is also warning. We stand in the brightness of His holiness. His searchlight focuses on us, revealing every flaw, every imperfection. When Christ, light in hand, makes His rounds from heart to heart, from house to house, what will He find? What sins will He expose with the light of His candle?

Yon house shows that in a temporal sense its occupants are well off. It is a beautiful, spacious, and gracious house, with many rooms and with a garage attached. The furnishings are the best. The house is equipped with every mechanical and electrical apparatus: electric dishwasher, automatic washing machine, color television, and every other means for convenient living. In the garage are several automobiles. These things are prestige symbols and impress people. What do they mean to God?

The Lord does not take great interest in status symbols. When He searches the house with candles, He looks for the people who occupy the house. What does He find when He examines them? Alas, behind outward riches He frequently finds deep spiritual poverty. Man may think: "I am rich and increased with goods and have need of nothing." God's inventory, on the other hand, may show that person to be "wretched and miserable and poor and blind and naked." The Lord may find no faith there, no love among the members of the family, no contentment with what He has provided, no peace of mind. Instead

[126]

He may find cares, anxieties, sorrows, and tensions. In a spiritual sense that house is bankrupt. We, too, should ask: How do things stand in our house? If the Lord were to visit us with His candles, what would He find?

The Word of God is sharp and piercing, like a searchlight penetrating to the heart. The heart is really the seat and dwelling place of the human being. What he is in his external life, that he was first of all in his heart. Not out of the head, eyes, mouth, or hands but "out of the *heart* proceed evil thoughts, murders, adulteries, fornications, thefts, false witness, blasphemies." Therefore we are above all concerned about what God finds in the heart. He sees all in the light of His omniscience. So the Scriptures teach: "Thou hast set our iniquities before Thee, our secret sins in the light of Thy countenance." Again: "Am I a God at hand, saith the Lord, and not a God afar off? Can any hide himself in secret places that I shall not see him? saith the Lord."

A soldier of World War I explained how he came out of the conflict sound in body and soul. He said, "I could not avoid being surrounded by evil companions. Many were the temptations the devil put in my way, but by God's help I did not succumb to them. I remembered in every instance the words: 'Thou, Lord, seest me.' My parents, brothers, sisters, friends, neighbors, and fellow Christians could not see what I was doing but God could. The remembrance of this truth kept me on the paths of purity."

In order that we may cleanse our way and walk uprightly in this world, God gave us His Word. His Word is the divine light on our life, not only as a searchlight but also as a guiding light.

II

God's Word as a Guiding Light

Wherever we may be or wherever we may go, for all we think, desire, speak, or do, God's Word is a lamp unto our feet and a light unto our path. Job also declares that "His candle shined upon my head" and "by His light I walked through darkness."

The Word of God is heavily underscored as a guiding light by the prophet Zephaniah, who writes: "The just Lord is in the midst thereof; He will not do iniquity; every morning doth He bring His judgment to light, He faileth not." Not a day passes in our lives but that God shows us His will and Word, His instructions and judgments. These, as the light of a bright candle, show us the right way.

Zephaniah writes further: "For then will I turn to the people a pure language, that they may all call upon the name of the Lord, to serve Him with one consent." Apart from declaring His holy will in the Law, it is evident that another kind of message is given. This is the word of comfort the Lord publishes through the mouth of His prophets. It is, also in Old Testament times, the Word of the Gospel.

The Lord has more to say through Zephaniah of the light of the Gospel, namely: "Sing, O daughter of Zion; shout, O Israel; be glad and rejoice with all the heart, O daughter of Jerusalem. The Lord hath taken away thy judgments, He hath cast out thine enemy; the King of Israel, even the Lord, is in the midst of thee: thou shalt not see evil anymore."

The light of the Gospel gives occasion for great joy because Christ is revealed as the Savior. Isaiah, a fellow prophet, writes: "The people that walked in darkness have seen a great light; they that dwell in the land of the shadow of death, upon them hath the light shined." He continues: "The joy before thee according to the joy in harvest, and as men rejoice when they divide the spoil." The reason for joy? The dominion of darkness is ended; the power of sin is broken. Christ is here, Christ the bright Morning Star, the Sun of Righeousness, the Light of the world. These prophecies were fulfilled with the coming of Jesus of Nazareth, as St. Matthew reports: "And leaving Nazareth, Jesus came and dwelt in Capernaum, which is upon the seacoast, in the borders of Zabulon and Nephthalim, that it might be fulfilled which was spoken by Esaias the prophet. . . ."

Why is the Gospel to be compared to a guiding light? Even the Law is for the righteous a light, polestar, plumb line, and rule for a God-pleasing life. Those are good works which believers do in faith, according to the Ten Commandments. The Law in its third use or function, namely, as a rule for God's children, can show us the life of righteousness but cannot give us power to attain that life, cannot guide us to eternal life. For this God gave a better light, the Gospel.

Where do we find the Gospel? Always and only in the Holy Scriptures. The written Word reveals the Gospel to us. All Scriptures, given by inspiration, "are able to make thee wise unto salvation through faith which is in Christ Jesus." The Bible teaches the Gospel, namely, that Christ is the only Way to eternal life. Man could not know this of his own reason or strength. Therefore God made a special revelation of this blessed truth in His Word. The Gospel teaches that Christ came into the world to save sinners; that His blood cleanses us from all sin. What the Gospel promises is dependable, for God stands behind His

Word down to the last jot and tittle. He who believes on Jesus Christ will be saved, as surely as heaven and earth exist.

The bright light of the Gospel shines in this sin-darkened world. Mankind, by nature spiritually blind, cannot see it. Also *we* could not have seen it unless God had given us spiritual sight. In order that we might see the light of God's love, the Holy Spirit kindled a light within us, namely faith. Through the eyes of faith we see the light. When the two lights meet, the light of the Gospel and the light of faith, we see clearly the way to eternal life and are enabled to walk this path. Now we are truly an enlightened people. We are like a ship's crew, in a dark and foggy night, able to see the lighthouse on the shore and to steer the vessel safely into harbor. As the star led the Wise Men of the East to Christ, so the polestar of the Gospel still guides us to the Savior.

May we always follow this light. Then we shall be lights in the Lord. First of all, we have the light *in us,* because faith was kindled in our hearts by the Holy Spirit. Through diligent use of the means of grace the flame of this light is fed and enabled to shine brightly. What our Savior said in another connection applies to the maintenance of the light within us: "Take heed therefore that the light which is in thee be not darkness. If thy whole body therefore be full of light, having no part dark, the whole shall be full of light, as when the bright shining of a candle doth give thee light."

Furthermore, if we are inwardly enlightened, the light will *shine outwardly* through us, to be seen by our fellowmen. It is Christ's will that those around us be attracted by this light, for He says: "Let your light so shine before men that they may see your

[130]

good works and glorify your Father which is in heaven." As long as we are in this world, God's Word, both as a searchlight and a guiding light, will shine in us and through us, unless, of course, we despise it and turn to human lights. Then God will remove the golden candlestick from our midst. On the other hand, if we appreciate and accept His light, God will ordain that the candlestick of the means of grace remain for us and for our children.

Finally there will come a time when we no longer need this light. Streetlamps are not needed in bright daylight because the sun is shining. En route to the Promised Land the Children of Israel were guided by a pillar of light. On arriving at their destination, this guiding light ceased. When once we have arrived in heaven, where we see God face to face and will have perfect understanding of God's gracious will, the light that guides us now will cease. Heaven will have its own light, as John writes: "There shall be no night there; and they need no candle, neither light of the sun; for the Lord God giveth them light; and they shall reign forever and ever."

May God bring us safely to this land of heavenly light!

HAGGAI

The Upkeep of Two Houses

Then came the Word of the Lord by Haggai the prophet, saying, Is it time for you, O ye, to dwell in your ceiled houses, and this house lie waste? Now therefore thus saith the Lord of hosts, Consider your ways. Ye have sown much and bring in little; ye eat, but ye have not enough; ye drink, but ye are not filled with drink; ye clothe you, but there is none warm; and he that earneth wages earneth wages to put it into a bag with holes. Thus saith the Lord of hosts, Consider your ways. Go up to the mountain and bring wood and build the house; and I will take pleasure in it, and I will be glorified, saith the Lord.

Haggai 1:3-8

IT IS CUSTOMARY for some urban dwellers to leave the city on weekends for their country cottages on lakes or in the mountains. Regrettably, these weekly excursions into rural areas, particularly in the summer, have a tendency to keep people away from Sunday worship. It need not be so, for owners of country homes can worship in nearby churches if they are so minded. The weekend trend from the city to the country reminds us of an opposite movement in an early German settlement in Texas. There many of the ranchers built themselves cottages in town, where the church was located. On Saturday afternoons they would occupy these town houses so that they might be on hand, refreshed and composed, for Sunday worship. It can be said that these early settlers in the Texas community established town homes for the express purpose of maintaining and supporting their spiritual home, the church. When the house of God is truly appreciated, people will arrange their personal, domestic, and vocational affairs in such a way that the maintenance of the church receives primary consideration. This is the lesson we learn from the prophet Haggai, who urges The Upkeep of Two Houses: (1) The believers' responsibility toward both houses; (2) the promise of divine blessing on both houses.

I

The Believers' Responsibility Toward Both Houses

Haggai lived and labored in the time after the return from Babylonian Exile. The people who resettled Jerusalem and the surrounding area began immediately to erect an altar, observe the feasts, and lay the foundation for a temple. Taking the leadership in these spiritual enterprises were Zerubbabel, governor of Judah, and Joshua, the high priest. When unfriendly neighbors, the native Samaritans, saw the intention of the Jews to build a permanent temple, they resolved on tactics to prevent the undertaking. The first attempt consisted in offering a pretended cooperation. The Jewish leaders saw through the scheme and promptly refused the proffered aid. The next step was more successful. The adversaries addressed themselves to the Persian kings, requesting the issuance of an injunction against the erection of the temple. From Artaxerxes they at long last managed to get a prohibition, which they gleefully published in Jerusalem, and thus "by force and power" they made the Jews stop the work. Ezra records:

[133]

"Then ceased the work of the house of God which is at Jerusalem. So it ceased unto the second year of the reign of Darius, king of Persia."

Some 18 years had now gone by, and nothing had been done to put the superstructure on the abandoned foundation. With a change of administration under Darius, two prophets, namely, Haggai and Zechariah, began to stir up interest in building the house of God. From God, Haggai received a series of four messages intended for Zerubbabel and Joshua. It is with the first of these divine revelations that we are now concerned. It told the two leaders: "Thus speaketh the Lord of hosts, saying, This people say, The time is now come, the time that the Lord's house shall be built." The people are not quoted as being opposed to the eventual completion of the temple. Their claim is that it is not an opportune time to do it now.

To this spirit of procrastination the prophet addresses himself. Referring to the "it is not the right time" excuse, he asks in return: "Is it time for you, O ye, to dwell in your ceiled houses, and this house lie waste?" To the extenuating plea: "The times are not good; we cannot afford to erect the temple now," Haggai reples with two considerations. In the first he points out the inconsistency of living in permanently constructed, interiorly finished, and well-furnished private homes while brambles are growing over the disintegrating temple foundation. In other words, the question must be asked: "If economic conditions forbid the construction of the Lord's sanctuary, how is it that you can afford ceiled, or wainscoted, houses for your own residence?"

Secondly, Haggai points out the price of neglecting the house of God. If for farmers there are crop failures due to drought and city workers' earnings do not accumulate because of inflation, is it not because God is withholding His blessing? It is not good stewardship practice, the prophet implies, to postpone the project because economic conditions are adverse. As long as the Lord's house lies neglected, temporal blessings will be withheld. Therefore the rallying cry, "Go up to the mountain and bring wood and build the house; and I will take pleasure in it, and I will be glorified, saith the Lord."

There is nothing in Haggai's message to suggest the Lord's disapproval of commodious private dwellings. While He would be displeased at wanton waste or lavish luxury intended to make the home a prideful status symbol, God is in favor of every measure taken to establish adequate housing for the family. The believers' home is a spiritual castle, a mighty fortress shielding the members of the household from the storms of life. Steps taken to strengthen the home and to make it attractive to the family certainly have God's approbation. It is indeed His will that we give attention to the domestic center, for it, too, is His house. The family altar, where prayers are spoken and parents conduct religious instruction, makes the home a true sanctuary where God's honor dwells. The family is God's little congregation, and its head is priest and provider. To provide suitable shelter for the family belongs to the sacred duties of the father. St. Paul states this truth bluntly: "If any provide not for his own, and especially for those of his own house, he has denied the faith and is worse than an infidel."

What, then, is at issue in Haggai's reference to ceiled houses? It is the fact of an imbalance, the fact that the Lord's house lies waste. The returned exiles in and about Jerusalem had not done wrong in build-

[135]

ing their own homes. Their mistake lay in something they had left undone. It was, after all, very important to their spiritual welfare to have a sanctuary, or a church home, where public worship could be conducted, the obligatory religious rites performed, religious instruction held, and the means of grace dispensed. The divinely ordained priesthood could not properly carry out its spiritual functions within the congregation if there was no temple. Without a temple the Word of God would be severely restricted in the conveyance of its blessings to city, community, and private home. Therefore Haggai felt constrained, as God's messenger, to lay upon the hearts of leaders and people the need of expediting the building of the Lord's house.

Haggai did not advocate a deed which God's people might regard as optional or as a matter of spiritual luxury. The believers of a given community are under the divine mandate to assemble for joint worship as part of sanctifying the Lord's day. Apart from the administration of the means of grace in public worship, no congregation can exist. The sanctuary, with its altar and other worship appointments, is a building which the congregation constructs and then consecrates to the glory and service of God. In interim periods it is possible to worship in temporary quarters, such as public halls, public schools, or vacant stores, but always with some loss to the spiritual edification of the flock. As a family needs a home, so the larger family that is the congregation needs a church home where it can offer up spiritual sacrifices. The church, where the household of God meets, is the focal point of love and devotion to God. To live in comfortable private homes but to let the temple lie waste bespeaks a serious lack in the zeal which God's people should have for His house.

[136]

Christian people, when establishing themselves in new communities, were as a rule responsive to the responsibility of building the Lord's house, as were also the people of Jerusalem when Haggai and Zechariah reminded them of their duty. When early Christian settlers in America had so much as a roof over their heads, they began at once to make plans for a church. Their churches were in many instances rough-hewn log structures, even as their own homes were of primitive simplicity. Nevertheless God was pleased to accept these unadorned temples as His dwelling places because they were the offerings of faith and represented the best His people could afford. Simple chapels though they were, He graced them with His presence, clothing them with a beauty far excelling the marbled splendor of cathedrals built more in pride than in humble faith. God honors every church which His children erect in recognition of their responsibility to worship Him in spirit and in truth.

II

The Promise of Divine Blessing on Both Houses

When man seeks first the kingdom of God and His righteousness, the things pertaining to his temporal sustenance will be added to him. The questions Jesus poses in the Sermon on the Mount as anxiously asked by many people: "What shall we eat?" "What shall we drink?" and "Wherewithal shall we be clothed?" were undoubtedly often raised in Jerusalem in the time of Haggai. There was "a drought upon the land and upon the mountains and upon the corn and upon the new wine and upon the oil and upon that which the ground bringeth forth." Why the lack of rain and shortages in necessary supplies? The Lord replied: "Because of Mine house that is waste."

[137]

The Lord's complaint implies a promise, namely, that with the removal of the cause of adversity His blessings would return. That is the way things turned out. In answer to the divine appeal communicated by Haggai the people of Jerusalem proved their faith and love by building the temple. Now blessings again abounded to relieve want. The seed sown developed into a good harvest to provide food and drink. Families brought home the yield of fields, gardens, and orchards. With food again in good supply, famine prices subsided. Earners no longer put their wages in bags full of holes. The inflation over, their money again had equitable purchasing power. Thus blessings were multiplied again on the community and its homes. The Lord's promise "I am with you" bespoke His gracious presence and power among His obedient people.

Those who love Zion always experience divine blessings on their houses. In Ps. 128 God promises: "Blessed is everyone that feareth the Lord, that walketh in His ways. For thou shalt eat the labor of thine hands; happy shalt thou be, and it shall be well with thee. Thy wife shall be as a fruitful vine by the sides of thine house; thy children like olive plants round about thy table. Behold that thus shall the man be blessed that feareth the Lord. The Lord shall bless thee out of Zion; and thou shalt see the good of Jerusalem all the days of thy life. Yea, thou shalt see thy children's children, and peace upon Israel." These words show how closely domestic bliss is intertwined with the family's right relationship to God. From His Zion, which is the church, God blesses private homes. There is, as it were, a channel from the Lord's house to individual houses, carrying the water of life from the divine fountain to all members of the family. The truths of the Word of God flow from church to home and bring peace. When parents and children love the habitation of God's house and the place where His honor dwelleth, they may rest assured that God will bless the home with temporal and spiritual endowments. There is no want in such a home, as the hymn verse declares,

> Blest such a house, it prospers well,
> In peace and joy the parents dwell,
> And in their children's lot is shown
> How richly God can bless His own.

Through Haggai, God also promised to multiply His blessings on the temple now being built. What God's house is not yet, it will become. Let leaders and people keep this in mind when they look on the present modest edifice. In beauty it could not compare with the glory of Solomon's temple, which was destroyed 586 B. C. At the time of dedication there might still have been elderly people who had childhood memories of the former temple. Ezra tells us that at the previous occasion, namely, the dedication of the foundation some 18 years before, some who had seen the preexilic temple "wept with a loud voice," the sound of their weeping mingling with the hymnal strains of joy. They could see by the outlines of the foundation that this temple would be inferior to Solomon's. Now that the new temple took definite shape, there may have been similar expressions of chagrin. Therefore Haggai asked: "Who is left among you that saw this house in her first glory? And how do ye see it now? Is it not in your eyes in comparison of it as nothing?"

The prophet would have the people see beyond the present building to the glorious future of the church of God. In a reference to the Messianic era

he foretold of the time when God would shake the
nations. The people, both Israelites and Gentiles,
would come from many countries and bear gifts to
enrich the Lord's house. This is also what Isaiah
foretold: "The multitude of camels shall cover thee,
the dromedaries of Midian and Ephah; all they from
Sheba shall come; they shall bring gold and incense;
and they shall show forth the praises of the Lord."
These prophecies began to be fulfilled when the
Wise Men of the East came to Jerusalem, presenting
to the newborn King of the Jews their gifts of gold,
frankincense, and myrrh. These gifts were the firstfruits of the "Desire of all nations" which would
glorify God's house. Thus "the glory of this latter
house shall be greater than of the former, saith the
Lord of hosts; and in this place will I give peace, saith
the Lord of Hosts."

Zerubbabel's temple was not final. It was in time
succeeded by the temple of Herod, which in turn
was destroyed A. D. 70. None of the material sanctuaries could do justice to the vision expressed by
Haggai of the future of God's church. Earthly structures are but symbols of a temple not made with
hands, namely, the New Testament Zion in the reign
of the Messiah. The church of Christ, as the divine
household in which Gentiles are fellow citizens with
the saints of Israel, is that better house whose glory
far excels the Old Testament fellowship. In the more
excellent communion of saints, Christ is our Peace,
having taken away the partition between Jews and
Gentiles when He reconciled both unto God by the
shedding of His blood. The Savior's words are thus
a blessing: "Peace I leave with you, My peace I give
unto you." In Christ we have peace with God based
on the forgiveness of sins, as Paul teaches: "Being

justified by faith, we have peace with God through our Lord Jesus Christ." How wonderful the promise of blessing on the whole church of God!

Jesus Christ, our Lord and Savior, loves all Christian homes, gracing them with His presence. He loved the church and gave Himself for it. From Him we learn to love both houses, ours and God's, keeping them true to their spiritual purpose. We recognize it as our Christian responsibility to maintain both institutions, home and church. And the consequence by God's grace? Shakespeare has one of his characters speak of a plague on both houses. God instead pronounces a blessing on both houses. Truly, "the Lord shall bless thee out of Zion, and thou shalt see the good of Jerusalem all the days of thy life."

ZECHARIAH

(Advent Message)

The Enthroned Priest

> *Take silver and gold, and make crowns, and set them upon the head of Joshua, the son of Josedech, the high priest; and speak unto him, saying, Thus speaketh the Lord of hosts, saying, Behold the man whose name is The BRANCH; and He shall grow up out of His place, and He shall build the temple of the Lord. Even He shall build the temple of the Lord; and He shall bear the glory, and shall sit and rule upon His throne; and He shall be a Priest upon His throne, and the counsel of peace shall be between them both.*
>
> *Zechariah 6:11-13*

IN A LAND LIKE OURS there are many interesting sights to see. The state of Colorado, to mention but one, abounds in faith-inspiring scenery. There are high mountains and green valleys, reminiscent of the poet's graphic words: ". . . purple mountain majesties above the fruited plain." If one wishes to view the surroundings from a high vantage point, he can ascend Pikes Peak and other, less-known but equally majestic, mountains. A totally different impression is gained from taking a train trip through the Royal Gorge, where the Arkansas River flows, and looking up to the highway bridge spanning the canyon some thousand feet overhead.

What do tourists say when they see these sights for the first time? They express admiration in such terms as "Wonderful!" "Inspiring!" or "Something like this we have not seen before!" If they are Christians, they will praise God for His marvelous work in nature.

Advent is a time of exclamations. Its announcement of the coming Christ incites admiration and wonder. The journey of faith, with prophets as tour directors, takes us through an exciting country: the Old Testament prophecies of the Messiah. What is so magnificently surprising is that God's prophets, hundreds of years before the birth of the Savior, implicitly and explicitly testify of Him whose name is Wonderful. Such a prophecy commends itself to our attention at this time. Zechariah invites us to admire The Enthroned Priest: (1) Why our faith admires this Priest; (2) how our admiration of Him turns to service.

I

Why Our Faith Admires This Priest

The prophet Zechariah is no stranger to the church as it contemplates the advent of the royal Messiah. It is he who prophesied: "Rejoice greatly, O daughter of Zion! Shout, O daughter of Jerusalem! Behold, thy King cometh unto thee; He is just and having salvation, lowly, and riding upon an ass, and upon a colt, the foal of an ass." To this Messianic text Zechariah adds another, namely, his prophecy of the coming Christ as both King and Priest.

This utterance is to be understood in the light of historical conditions prevailing at the time of Zechariah. The time was approximately 500 B.C., the era following the Babylonian Captivity. A representative part of God's people had returned to Palestine to repossess the land and restore Jerusalem. The leaders of this resettlement project had their minds mostly on the secular pursuit of rebuilding the city walls. All the while the Lord's house continued to lie waste. It remained for the prophets Haggai and Zechariah to urge both leaders and people to build the temple and revive sanctuary worship. This is Zechariah's task. Through plain speech, visions, and a series of symbolical acts the prophet strove to arouse interest in God's spiritual purpose among His people.

On this occasion there was present in Jerusalem a committee of Jews from Babylon with a gift of gold and silver. In Babylon many Jews had acquired considerable wealth through commercial enterprises. They did not desire to leave their prosperous positions in Babylon and become pioneers in Palestine. While remaining in what was now their home country, they nevertheless supported the resettlement of the Holy Land with generous donations, the way American Zionists did in modern times.

The Word of the Lord directed Zechariah to accept the gold and silver from the delegation, make of them two crowns, and set them on the head of the high priest, whose name was Joshua. The name *Joshua* ("Jehovah is salvation") has the same meaning as the name *Jesus* ("He shall save His people from their sins"). Joshua, wearing the royal and sacerdotal crowns, was a type of the Messiah, who likewise was anointed to be our King and Priest.

By the Word of God, Zechariah was instructed to say to Joshua, the doubly crowned high priest: "Behold the man whose name is The BRANCH; and He shall grow up out of His place, and He shall build the temple of the Lord." This important message is emphatically repeated in the following verse: "Even

[144]

He shall build the temple of the Lord; and He shall bear the glory, and shall sit and rule upon His throne; and He shall be a Priest upon His throne, and the counsel of peace shall be between them both."

All of this had Messianic significance. Beyond the immediate historical situation there is an implicit prophecy here of the advent of the Son of God as ultimate Peacemaker between God and mankind. Joshua is indeed a picture of the true High Priest, Jesus Christ. Similarly, the as yet unfinished earthly temple in Jerusalem is a type of the spiritual temple not made with hands, namely, the New Testament church which Christ built.

Who is the amazing high priest standing head and shoulders above Joshua? He is described as having a true human nature, for He is of human extraction. His descent from antecedent human stock is indicated in the name *The Branch*. Earlier (3:8) the prophet had said to Joshua, again speaking of a great high priest other than himself: "I will bring forth My Servant, the BRANCH."

We note how remarkably Zechariah's testimony coincides with that of Isaiah, who likewise had prophesied of the Messiah as the Servant of Jehovah in these words: "There shall come forth a Rod out of the stem (or stump) of Jesse, and a Branch shall grow out of his roots" (11:1). In his classic Messianic chapter, the 53d, Isaiah repeated the same truth: "He shall grow up before Him as a tender plant and as a root out of a dry ground." As a third witness, Jeremiah (23:5) adds: "Behold, the days come, saith the Lord, that I will raise unto David a righteous Branch, and a King shall reign and prosper, and shall execute judgment and justice in the earth."

[145]

There can be no doubt that Jesus of Nazareth, Scion of the tribe of Judah and of "the house and lineage of David," is the Branch springing from the root of Jesse. The family tree of Jesse and his son David was eventually reduced to a stump, but there is still life in it. Out of it sprouts a new twig, a branch, growing into a tree to shelter all nations. This Branch is Jesus Christ, indeed, as far as His human nature is concerned, of Hebrew ancestry, as Paul testifies: ". . . made of the seed of David according to the flesh" (Rom. 1:3). Jesse, David, and their descendants are "the fathers, and of whom as concerning the flesh Christ came" (Rom. 9:5). The Messiah is, of course, also the Son of God, as Paul hastens to add: "Declared to be the Son of God with power," and "He is over all, God blessed forever."

Our faith admires the God-man, not only because of His two natures but also because of the dual offices He holds. Zechariah declares: "He shall be a Priest," indeed an extraordinary Priest because He is also a King. He is not a scion of the tribe of Levi, whence the priests regularly came, but of the royal tribe of Judah. In this anomaly He is like Abraham's contemporary, Melchizedek, king of Salem and priest of the Most High God, who also was not of Levitical lineage. He is, after the example of others before Him, a Priest who is also a crowned King.

Arousing our admiration even more is the fact that this Priest, in the discharge of His office, is willing to take upon Himself what is most unpleasant and ignominious. It is a pleasant privilege for a priest to wear a crown, bear the glory, and sit and rule upon his throne. But He is willing to assume also difficult tasks, specifically the task of building the temple. This is a temple not made with hands, the heavenly sanctuary, where man is reconciled to God. In entering

[146]

the holy of holies, the Messiah, as both Priest and Victim, must take upon Himself the most painful task of bringing an offering for sin. What was this offering? Indeed not a sacrifice of the blood of oxen, bullocks, or calves, but of His own blood. The Priest is simultaneously the Lamb of God slain for the sins of mankind. This Gospel truth is plainly taught by Isaiah, the most prominent of the Old Testament evangelists, who wrote: "The Lord hath laid on Him the iniquity of us all. He was oppressed, and He was afflicted, yet He opened not His mouth. He is brought as a lamb to the slaughter, and as a sheep before her shearers is dumb, so He openeth not His mouth." It was thus — through self-sacrifice — that the Priest was to build the temple of the Lord.

What an admirable High Priest! In the New Testament we see Him in the clearer light of fulfillment. The author of the Epistle to the Hebrews identifies Jesus as the High Priest, ultimate, unique, and superior to all His fellows. He states: "Such an High Priest became us who is holy, harmless, undefiled, separate from sinners, and made higher than the heavens; who needeth not daily, as those high priests, to offer up sacrifice, first for His own sins and then for the people's; for this He did once when He offered up Himself." To make absolutely sure that the identity of this High Priest be not lost amid the use of pronouns, he expressly writes: ". . . we have a great High Priest that is passed into the heavens, Jesus, the Son of God."

Our faith must thus exclaim: What a royal Priest! He came, not to be ministered unto but to minister, and to give His life a ransom for the sins of all men. But there is in all this also a somber note that must be sounded. The height to which faith ascends in its appreciation of Christ stands in contrast to the depth of sin. Man's transgression was for Christ the vale of sweat, blood, and tears. Isaiah, in ch. 40, describes sin both graphically and geographically as uneven terrain consisting of the valleys of dejection and the mountains of pride; of crooked paths to be straightened and rough places to be made plain. Much spiritual road grading needs to be done in the desert of the human heart in order to prepare a highway for our God.

During this season we confess our many transgressions. We must not let the many activities of pre-Christmas weeks divert our thoughts from the reality of sin. The commercial world seeks to usher in the "Christmas spirit" with great clamor in the marketplace, thus disturbing the quiet, deeply spiritual, and penitent mood of Advent. The Christian will not let himself be stampeded into the kind of distraction that confuses Advent with a shallow Christmas concept. During Advent it is not yet time for the joy and jubilation of Christmas and to sing "Silent Night" or "Hark, the Herald Angels Sing!" The Advent season instead calls for repentance and for a due sense of sinfulness and unworthiness. It focuses on Jesus Christ, the High Priest who offered Himself for our sins, and thus prepares the heart for a worthy observance of His birth.

II

Our Admiration Turns to Service

If in faith we have marveled at this royal Priest, we cannot but turn our admiration to consecrated service. This is a second truth to be derived from the prophecy: "He shall be a Priest upon His throne."

Implied in the statement that the Messiah shall sit and rule upon His throne is the truth that we are

the subjects over whom He rules. We are the servants
of the Servant. How do we as an obedient people
serve Him? The Lord Jesus, whom we recognize as
the Messiah, is no longer on earth in the flesh to lay
stone on stone and thus to build the New Testament
temple. Nevertheless the work goes on because we,
as the members of His body, function in His behalf.
In continuous fulfillment of the prophecy "He shall
build the temple of the Lord" the Messiah employs
us, our hands, feet, mind, voice, and all personal
resources, for the furtherance of His kingdom. We
are involved with Christ in the building of His temple
when we witness for Him, proclaim His Gospel, and
preach His Word to the joy and edifying of His
people. When the Holy Spirit through our testimony
converts a sinner here, reclaims a backslider there;
here restores a fallen publican and there breaks down
a Pharisee in his pride and self-righteousness and
brings him to rely on Christ's righteousness, there is
in every instance another stone laid for the ultimate
completion of God's holy temple. Then the great
sacrifice of Christ comes to fruition. Then also more
people for whom Christ died become lively stones
in the edifice that is the holy Christian church.

There is a further service we render to the enthroned Priest. We minister to Him with our gifts,
saying, "Take my silver and my gold, Not a mite
would I withhold." Mention was made earlier of
pious Jews who had achieved prosperity in Babylon
and brought an offering of gold and silver. We, too,
bring as love offerings to the Lord our treasures great
and small. In doing so it is not at all our thought
to make a down payment or to effect an outright
purchase of our salvation. Not even Jesus Christ could
purchase and win us with gold or silver. Much less
can we ourselves do this. Not the labors of our hands,

not the love offerings of our hands, not even the largess of the proportion of a king's ransom could gain us peace with God. We are redeemed completely by the blood of Christ as of a Lamb without blemish and without spot. Only because He as our Substitute paid the uttermost farthing can we have the assurance of full and free forgiveness. Only the perfected work of Jesus Christ can be the basis of faith. Trust in the merits of the Savior yields a faith not only of validity but also of vitality. The living faith in Christ bears fruit, indeed much fruit in appreciation of all Christ has done. Included in the fruit of faith is the gladsome giving of the firstfruits of our labors, our offerings of gold and silver for the upbuilding of God's spiritual temple.

We render service to the royal Priest also with the sacrifice of our lips. Immaterial though they be, our praises and thanksgivings are offerings brought in faith and thus well pleasing to God. The prophet wrote of the heavenly Priest: "He shall bear the glory." Indeed, as King and Priest He is all-glorious, for His is the kingdom and the power and the glory. This fact we acknowledge when in psalms, hymns, and spiritual songs we give all glory to Him. Psalm 24 tells us what glory is due our Advent King and how we may render our tribute to Him. We are told: "Lift up your heads, O ye gates; and be ye lifted up, ye everlasting doors; and the King of Glory shall come in. Who is this King of Glory? The Lord strong and mighty, the Lord mighty in battle."

We serve the kingly Priest when we lend support to His peace program on earth. Zechariah did prophesy: "The counsel of peace shall be between them both." The Messiah came to effect man's reconciliation with God. He is thus the Counselor and Prince of Peace whom Isaiah extolled. The peace in heaven which He established becomes "peace on earth," not only in its prime meaning as spiritual peace with God but also as peace and goodwill toward men. Our Lord Himself in the Sermon on the Mount pronounced all peacemakers as "blessed." We serve Him when we seek and pursue peace in church, city, community, and world. Current animosities among nations and tensions among various race groups confront all of Christ's followers with the challenge to be His peace corps. The promotion of the "counsel of peace" is a noble service to Him who in Paul's words "is our Peace."

Zechariah speaks of two crowns for the coming Messiah as Priest and King. The honor that is His He is willing to share with us, His brethren. He "hath made us kings and priests unto God and His Father," John declares in the opening verses of Revelation. What a privilege it is for us to be elevated to this high position! May it remind us of two truths: first, as members of the royal priesthood we are privileged to "offer up spiritual sacrifices, acceptable to God by Jesus Christ." The second truth is that we are participants not only in honor but also in shame and suffering. As coregents with the enthroned Priest we must also suffer with Him, but by virtue of our union with Him our crosses are much easier to bear. We are humbly grateful for being considered worthy to partake of both His honor and dishonor. This is what Paul bids us remember in our relation to Christ: "If so be that we suffer with Him, that we may be also glorified together."

MALACHI

The Sun, the Satellite, and the Stars

> For, behold, the day cometh that shall burn as an oven; and all the proud, yea, and all that do wickedly, shall be stubble; and the day that cometh shall burn them up, saith the Lord of hosts, that it shall leave them neither root nor branch. But unto you that fear My name shall the Sun of Righteousness arise with healing in His wings; and ye shall go forth and grow up as calves of the stall. And ye shall tread down the wicked; for they shall be ashes under the soles of your feet in the day that I shall do this, saith the Lord of hosts. Remember ye the Law of Moses, My servant, which I commanded unto him in Horeb for all Israel, with the statutes and judgments. Behold, I will send you Elijah, the prophet, before the coming of the great and dreadful day of the Lord. And he shall turn the heart of the fathers to the children and the heart of the children to their fathers, lest I come and smite the earth with a curse.

Malachi 4:1-6

WHEN WEATHER REPORTS are given for the ensuing day, it is customary to say also when the sun rises and sets. Weather forecasts are subject to unpredictable changes. It is not so with announcements concerning sunrise and sunset. These future events can be calculated exactly, and that because God in the beginning ordained exact orbits and functions for the celestial bodies. On the fourth day of creation week

God said: "Let there be lights in the firmament of the heaven to divide the day from the night; and let them be for signs and for seasons and for days and years." The account continues thus: "And God made two great lights: the greater light to rule the day, and the lesser light to rule the night; He made the stars also." Since that time sun, moon, and stars in their orderly courses provide light for our natural lives in this world.

What is more, God provided, and still provides, light for our *spiritual* life, as St. Paul writes: "God, who commanded the light to shine out of darkness, hath shined in our hearts to give the light of the knowledge of the glory of God in the face of Jesus Christ." This truth is in essence also stated in our text. Reference is made to the source of spiritual light, the witness to this light, and the power of it in believers' lives. The instruction given through Malachi may be set forth thus: The Sun, the Satellite, and the Stars: (1) Christ, as the Sun of Righteousness, radiates the light of God and imparts healing; (2) John the Baptist, as the Sun's satellite, bears witness to the Light; (3) the believers, as stars in God's right hand, exemplify the blessings of the light.

I

Christ, as the Sun of Righteousness, Radiates the Light of God and Imparts Healing

The Son of God, who is to come as Messiah, is the Sun of Righteousness enlightening and healing us. We note how this is stated in the text: "But unto you that fear My name shall the Sun of Righteousness arise with healing in His wings." Of the natural sun the Savior once said that God makes it rise on the evil and on the good. That can also be said of the spiritual Sun. In the opening verse of this chapter God declares through the prophet: "For, behold, the day cometh that shall burn as an oven; and all the proud, yea, and all that do wickedly, shall be stubble; and the day that cometh shall burn them up, saith the Lord of hosts, that it shall leave them neither root nor branch." In the Messiah's day, which is the New Testament era, unbearable heat and consuming fire shall come as a judgment on the wicked. Divine wrath is here likened to intense bake-oven heat, to a forest fire burning up trees to roots and twigs, to a merciless sun beating down on hapless desert travelers. Yes, God makes the Sun of Righteousness rise also on the evil, not in providential kindness which prompts Him to spread natural sunshine abroad, but in judgment.

As far as God's children are concerned, the Sun rises for a different purpose. The words "but unto you" indicate the contrast, being addressed to those "that fear My name." The latter are the children of God, who believe on the Son of God and trust in His salvation. On them the Sun shall rise for their good. Who is the benefactor named the "Sun"? He is certainly the Messiah. So Zacharias, the father of John the Baptist, understood the meaning. In his song of praise, the *Benedictus*, he associates salvation, forgiveness of sins, and the tender mercy of God with "the Dayspring from on high." He said this in clear reference to the Messiah, whom he calls "an horn of salvation for us in the house of His servant David."

Christ is rightly called the *Sun*, for He is the Light of the world. He is the Light that came into the world to enlighten all men. He reveals the Father's love and the way of salvation. These truths are hid

[154]

from man's natural understanding, but Christ has now brought them to light. Now that the Sun has risen and the Holy Spirit has enlightened our hearts, we no longer stumble in the dark but walk in the light of God's Word.

Christ is the Sun of *Righteousness*. This expression is to be taken together with the testimony of Jeremiah, which reads: "This is His name whereby He shall be called, THE LORD OUR RIGHTEOUS-NESS." What righteousness is meant? The truth of Christ's personal righteousness, or the fact that He is in His own being altogether holy and sinless, does not afford consolation to sinners. Consolation comes only when Christ's righteousness is declared to be *their* righteousness, and is imparted to them as such. That is how the apostles expounded the doctrine of Christ's righteousness for us. Paul teaches that God "hath made Him to be sin for us who knew no sin, that we might be made the righteousness of God in Him." Peter joins him in saying: "Who His own self bare our sins in His own body on the tree, that we, being dead to sins, should live unto righteousness; by whose stripes ye were healed."

The sun has extended rays and beams which, in poetic comparison, resemble outstretched wings. In these wings there is healing. The light of the sun is a preventive against disease germs. It has healing qualities for sick bodies. That is why a hospital is equipped with a solarium, a room for the administration of sun baths. Christ, as the Sun of Righteousness, likewewise imparts healing. He is the Physician of the soul, forgiving iniquities and healing diseases. Isaiah prophesied that the Messiah was to come "to bind up the brokenhearted."

Jesus of Nazareth applied Isaiah's prophecy to

[155]

Himself. He told the disciples of John the Baptist that, by virtue of His ministry, "the blind receive their sight and the lame walk, the lepers are cleansed and the deaf hear, the dead are raised up, and the poor have the Gospel preached unto them." In ministering to the whole man, our Lord in many instances effected bodily healings. Yet it was not His primary mission to be a physical healer. The healing He came to impart was for sick souls, namely, forgiveness of sins. What He said to the man sick of the palsy He says to all who come to Him, mourning their sins, namely: "Be of good cheer, your sins are forgiven you." Christ had the authority to forgive sins because He Himself died on the cross in full atonement for them. The health of soul that lies in forgiveness is a gift that only He can give. As Peter declared, only in His name is there salvation.

In summary, Christ is the Sun of Righteousness who enlightens and heals. He is, to refer again to the creation of the natural sun, the great Light that rules the day. He is, according to John's repeated witness, the true Light, the incarnate Word full of grace and truth.

II

John the Baptist, as the Sun's Satellite, Bears Witness to the Light

God in the beginning created also a lesser light to function in close relation to the greater light, namely, the moon. This satellite, shining with reflected sunlight, is at once reminiscent of John the Baptist. John's mission was to precede the Dayspring from on high and to bear witness to the true Light.

John the Baptist, so our Lord Himself declared, was "a burning and a shining light." What kind of

[156]

light was he? Not the true Light, not the Sun of Righteousness, but second luminary comparable to the moon. God has something very definite to say in the text about John as forerunner. He declares: "Behold, I will send you Elijah, the prophet, before the coming of the great and dreadful day of the Lord." The original Elijah was a prophet living in the days of King Ahab. When his work on earth was completed, God took him bodily to heaven in a fiery chariot. At the dawn of the Messianic era there was to come a second Elijah, that is, a man of God in the spirit, power, and zeal of the first Elijah, and that was John the Baptist. We have the word of Jesus Himself for this identification: "For all the prophets and the Law prophesied until John. And if ye will receive it, this is Elias, which was for to come."

The prophecy of the coming of John is stated earlier in the Book of Malachi, namely, in the opening verse of the third chapter, where also the prophecy is introduced with an attention-arresting "behold!" The passage reads: "Behold, I will send My messenger, and he shall prepare the way before Me. And the Lord whom ye seek shall suddenly come to His temple, even the Messenger of the Covenant, whom ye delight in."

John was to come that he might prepare the way of the Messiah in a very special sense, namely, by enlightening and teaching the people. He was a witness to the Light, and most effective was his teaching and witnessing ministry. In every sense was fulfilled the prophecy that "he shall turn the heart of the fathers to the children and the heart of the children to their fathers." John had the assignment to turn the people to God. This required him to be a preacher of repentance, calling for the confession of sins and

[157]

the removal of all iniquity. Beyond preaching repentance, John pointed to Jesus Christ as the Lamb of God bearing the world's sin and bringing salvation. This testimony many of John's hearers took to heart, and thus they were reunited with God. From this it followed that they were also reconciled and reunited with one another in all human relationships, particularly the interpersonal relationships in the family.

John always directed men's thoughts to Christ, knowing full well that Christ is the Son of God and Redeemer, and he His witness. Christ is the Sun of Righteousness, and he His spiritual satellite. Christ was to run an eternal course, but he a limited, timely orbit. When came the time that the Sun had risen and the day of the Lord had fully come, there was no more need for the moon. This John realized, declaring: "He must increase, but I must decrease." Nevertheless, in view of his relation to Christ, John was an important light in his time. Our Lord Himself pays him this tribute: "Among them that are born of women there hath not risen a greater than John the Baptist."

III

The Believers, as Stars in God's Right Hand,
Exemplify the Blessings of the Light

In 1 Cor. 15 Paul writes: "There is one glory of the sun, and another glory of the moon, and another glory of the stars." We have spoken of the glory of Christ as the Sun and of John as His satellite. Who are we, and what is our position and function? If we make the third comparison, there is this to say: The believers, as stars in God's right hand, exemplify the blessings of the light.

Christians are also light. Paul says so expressly

in Philippians: "Be blameless and harmless, the sons of God, without rebuke, in the midst of a crooked and perverse nation, among whom ye shine as lights in the world." The Savior likewise instructed us to let our light shine before men. We are lights only because the Holy Spirit has through the Gospel enlightened us. Not only *in* us but also *through* us the light now shines. In our entire life and conversation we show the power and blessedness of the light. On what is this enlightened life of a Christian conditioned?

Christ would have us let our light shine that men may see our good works. What are good works? What is the good life that comes about when the Christian's desires, thoughts, words, and works are totaled up? A good work is what a child of God does in faith according to a divine norm, namely, the Ten Commandments. To be at all able to follow the divine norm, we must know what it is, what it contains, what it enjoins. Thus God declares through Malachi: "Remember ye the Law of Moses, My servant, which I commanded unto him in Horeb for all Israel, with the statutes and judgments." The Word of God is given us for our guidance, as the psalmist has said: "Thy Word is a lamp unto my feet and a light unto my path." In Ps. 19 it is pointed out how valuable the Law is that God once gave to all His people through Moses: "The Law of the Lord is perfect, converting the soul; the testimony of the Lord is sure, making wise the simple." Thus what the heavens declare through sun, moon, and stars in their orbits is much more plainly revealed through the Word in its constant going forth into the world.

As stars in God's right hand we exemplify not only the light but also the power of the Sun of righteousness. The natural sun abounds in chemical and physical energy, and this energy can be harnessed.

Likewise from the spiritual Sun, namely, Christ, comes power enabling us to be, to do, and to go according to His will. The prophet writes in the text: "And ye shall go forth," indeed go forth for Him into all the world and preach His Gospel.

What is more, sunlight contains power to facilitate growth, not only in the plant world but also in the animal kingdom. Without the sun young animals could not grow, flourish, and be nourished. Thanks to the light of Christ, we also grow in our spiritual lives — in faith and all good works. This is told in the text by an analogy from animal husbandry: Ye shall "grow up as calves of the stall."

Christians exemplify the blessing of the light also in their relation to the darkness of sin, to the spiritual night that enshrouds a hostile world. In our battle against the forces of darkness we shall win the victory, overcoming sin in us as well as the Satan and the world. The victory of the children of light is proclaimed in these words of the text: "Ye shall tread down the wicked; for they shall be ashes under the soles of your feet in the day that I shall do this, saith the Lord of hosts."

The message God communicates through Malachi in these verses constitutes the last chapter of the Old Testament. The prophecy of the Sun of Righteousness and its secondary lights forms the bridge to the New Testament and the full Gospel there proclaimed. While the words of Malachi here are Messianic, they also reveal the sharpness of the Law and the threat of divine wrath. The Old Testament as Malachi concluded it ends in a curse: "lest I come and smite the earth with a curse." With that compare the last words in the Book of Revelation, which pronounces a blood-curdling warning and curse (Rev. 22:18, 19) against those that tamper with God's Word, and then closes with this gracious promise and blessing for all true believers: "The grace of our Lord Jesus Christ be with you all." How thankful we should be that God fulfilled His promise to send the Sun of Righteousness! Now that the true Light has come, we behold the glory of the only-begotten Son of God, full of grace and truth.

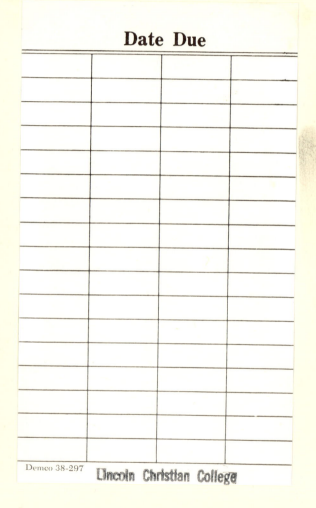